simply fish

HEALTHY, SEASONAL, AND SUSTAINABLE SEAFOOD

Matthew Dolan

Photography by Anne-Claire Thieulon

Skyhorse Publishing

Skyhorse Publishing books may be purchased in bulk at special discounts for sales promotion, corporate gifts, fund-raising, or educational purposes. Special editions can also be created to specifications. For details, contact the Special Sales Department, Skyhorse Publishing, 307 West 36th Street, 11th Floor, New York, NY 10018 or info@skyhorsepublishing.com.

Skyhorse® and Skyhorse Publishing® are registered trademarks of Skyhorse Publishing, Inc.®, a Delaware corporation.

Visit our website at www.skyhorsepublishing.com.

10 9 8 7 6 5 4 3 2 1

Library of Congress Cataloging-in-Publication Data is available on file.

Cover design by Daniel Brount
Cover photo by Anne-Claire Thieulon

Hardcover ISBN: 978-1-5107-1750-3
Paperback ISBN: 978-1-5107-5251-1
Ebook ISBN: 978-1-5107-1751-0

Printed in China

Praise for *Simply Fish*

"I see a lot of cookbooks. I recommend few. It is in that context that I heartily recommend *Simply Fish* by Chef Matthew Dolan. The book is beautifully designed and photographed. Its seasonal organization is unique and smart. Most importantly, Matthew's culinary expertise and clear writing serves to demystify the cooking of fish for the non-professional."
—Dr. Tim Ryan, president of The Culinary Institute of America

"*Simply Fish* is your definitive guide to preparing seafood that is sustainable, healthy, and delicious. Matthew Dolan's recipes are accessible and brilliant, and his stories are engaging. The bounty of the sea is here, in a book you'll treasure."
—Drew Nieporent, restaurateur, Tribeca Grill, Nobu, Bâtard

"A masterful, authoritative walk from the piers to the fish counter and into your kitchen, Dolan shares his favorite recipes to lead us in the sustainable and delicious world of seafood. Beyond the scrumptious recipes, his tips for how to talk with your local fishmonger is empowering both for home cooks and chefs alike."
—Rob Connoley, owner of Bulrush STL, author of *Acorns & Cattails*

"I am absolutely delighted to find my boundless enthusiasm for seafood freshness is shared by Chef Dolan. His latest book *Simply Fish* is both a fine tribute to fresh seafood and a practical guide for anyone who wants to do it yourself at home. In addition to page after page of mouthwatering recipes, there is a trove of information, tips, and questions that a shopper and home cook can ask at the market. For fish lovers everywhere, *Simply Fish* is simply great!"
—Chef Martin Yan, host of *Yan Can Cook*

"A great collection of recipes and stories to inspire us all to eat more seafood at home. Matt's seasonal sensibility, attention to detail, and commitment to sustainability are what sets this book apart from all the cookbooks on your shelf. Using these recipes will ensure our grandkids have a variety of healthful seafood, too!"
—Mary Sue Milliken, celebrity chef and restaurateur

for my Mom, Carol Dolan

Thank you for your cooking, your amazing sense of humor, for tolerating the late night rants once upon a time, and for believing in me along the way.

contents

part 1

introduction / ix

why fish? / xi

sustainability / xiii

q&a with crystal sanders / xv

getting started / xix

part 2

winter / 1

spring / 49

summer / 99

fall / 139

the whole fish and larger gatherings / 181

about the author / 183

acknowledgments / 184

resources / 185

glossary of terms / 186

index / 195

Part 1

introduction

Americans are eating more fish. Thank God! Because fish is a healthier and more sustainable meat alternative, more steak junkies are migrating over to the proteins from the sea. Please pardon my hypocrisy, as I am a lover of steak as well, but the truth is, any of us living near a single body of healthy water have inherited generations upon generations of seafood dishes. These deeply-rooted cultural delicacies have undergone the passage of time and are still well-entrenched in our day-to-day lives. My own culinary exploration through a few corners of the United States and parts of Western Europe confirmed that no matter where you are, fish is on the menu.

I am an American, aware of my Celtic roots, and I blame these roots for the passion that I carry forth in all things, especially my love of cooking and creating dynamic experiences through food. Cooking for others is a joy rewarded by seeing the enjoyment of others. Passion and care are the fundamentals of excellent food, and I am passionate about fish. We should eat more of it. It turns out, one billion people rely upon fish as their primary source of protein, so welcome to my collection of stories and recipes showcasing how we can cook great fish for ourselves and our friends, and how we can simplify the entire process to enjoy delicious meals focused on seafood.

In this book, we will explore a wide variety of fish recipes, prepping techniques, and tricks that will lead to memorable experiences and culinary creations simply through cooking fish. I will give you tips on what to ask the guy at the fish counter and what they can do to make your prep list a bit lighter (they won't love me for this, but you will!) so that you can deliver a restaurant quality experience in your own home—either for yourself or the twenty people that followed you home from work that day! Unlikely, but you see my point.

Whether you are entertaining or simply want to eat a trout and listen to Mozart by yourself while sipping a glass of white wine and navigating the trout's fiddly bones, this book is for you. I will walk you through the steps of a variety of different fish options for each season, as well as a few desserts (please note that no fish will be used in the making of any dessert offerings). The recipes will vary from casual and quick to more advanced and adventuresome, and will simply demystify the entire process. So please, have fun at your own event, enjoy amazing fish and some time out of the kitchen (let's be honest, you are still cooking for people so we are going to make this as painless as possible), and have fun cooking healthy and delicious fish.

Let's dive into simply cooking fish!

why fish?

The desire to write this book was to see fish back in the home kitchen. For those of you who cannot cook fish with great confidence, you now have a new resource that will not only help you cook fish, but will show you how to create beautiful accompaniments to complete the meal, and guide you toward sustainable offerings (as with all food, we should care where our fish comes from and purchase responsibly). That may seem like a last minute message, but conserving our great resources from the sea is all of our responsibility.

Another main reason is that fish are loaded with omega-3 fatty acids that lower bad cholesterol or low density lipids, which are a major contributor to heart conditions. Omegas 3s are also recognized as carriers of good cholesterol through our circulatory system, which hunt the bad cholesterol while lowering our risk of heart attack and stroke—as though we needed another reason to eat fish!

The final message I want to send is simple. It is simply that fish is delicious and good for you. If you are like most people, you want little part in preparing fish for others, but now you can—in a quick, easy, and delicious way. Hide this book when they come over and take full credit for your delicious seafood feast.

You've earned it!

sustainability

I recently learned about Crappie . . . a type of fish with a terrible name. I spoke with a fisherman buddy who explained they are everywhere in lake and river systems both in the Northeast and in California. This chat shed further light on the sad reality that not enough people live near the sea. Not enough people share a sunrise or sunset, and not enough people know how to cook fish. Here in northern California, Crappie fish exist in cesspool lakes and ponds and are laden with mercury; and yet, people still eat it. It's an all-you-can-eat buffet. Okay, I'll chill out for a moment, but I really do want to help people eat more fish at home. It's not that scary, smelly, nor challenging.

When I moved back to the US from Finland, a Northern European country that wouldn't serve crappie fish to their worst prisoners, I embraced a new respect and understanding for the lesser known fishes. I learned how to make the best out of them, and how to work them into menus in great restaurants where folks were not married to the tunas and salmons. We are not going to go that route here; instead, this book is in print to help you make better choices. If you are still reading, then you clearly will eat a piece of fish . . . great start! Now, maybe you live in my old New York City apartment where there isn't any room to cut fish and the trash can's next to your pillow. If that's remotely close, this book offers recipes that will guide you through the fish counter to the guys with the gloves and the knives that will clean, scale, and portion whatever you want—you just need to ask.

This could get very preachy, so let's get that part out of the way for now. We must care about the origin of our food. The planet is getting crowded and we are consuming more than ever. Fishing regulations are questionable on all continents, and if a fish isn't caught with a rod and reel by a guy whose name you know, question it. Yes, this is next to impossible, so the plan here is to not only showcase easy-to-execute recipes, but to also give you some helpful tips to select good choices, ask for a ready-to-cook option from your local store, and navigate this slightly daunting process.

Before we jump into this, let's briefly identify why this is important. To me, it's clear that fish is a healthier source of protein. I love steaks and burgers so much that I opened a burger restaurant in 2014, but if we could all choose a fish option over a meat option once a week, we would be able to reduce the methane emission created by the cattle and beef industry. Currently, their negative effect is greater than that of the automobile industry. Sorry, it's getting preachy again. On a more positive note, and what I will say forever and possibly have a few posters made on the topic, eating fish lets you live longer, makes you much more interesting, stops hair loss, prevents gingivitis, and actually straightens your teeth while making you sexier if that is even possible. Okay, it is very good for you. It's also delicious, so let's do this!

q&a with crystal sanders

marine biologist and founder of fish revolution

While it is clear that I am not a scientist, I want my kids to be able to enjoy the same great stuff from the sea that I enjoyed as a kid, so I thought I should ask a real scientist some questions to make this point actually tangible. I reached out to an old colleague and new friend, Crystal Sanders, who is a marine biologist and founder of Fish Revolution. There are few folks out there who have the same up-to-date knowledge and passion as she, and here's what she had to say.

Why do you care about ocean issues and why should we?

Growing up along the Gulf Coast, I developed an early love of the ocean. My Grandpa used to take me fishing on our weekend trips to visit my great-grandmother, and I was always fascinated by whatever was coming up on the hook. Even if it was not something we could eat, I just wanted to know what was under the water. I knew at a young age that I wanted to be a Marine Biologist, and wasn't quite sure where that would lead me career-wise. I just knew I loved science and I loved the ocean. I have spent most of my adult life engaging with the ocean. I really find it magnificent from just sitting on the beach watching the waves roll in with such consistency, yet so dynamic, as well. I have been fortunate enough to be able to log many hours onboard boats out in the water and scuba diving under the water's surface. It's unbelievably inspiring to immerse yourself in the underwater world in such a vulnerable way, you know, strapped to a metal tank of air as your only underwater life support. It's like an entirely different universe under the waves. A big, blue, beautiful universe. There is no way I could not dedicate myself to doing everything in my power to protect the ocean after experiencing so much of its beauty.

I know that mankind has done some damage to our oceans, to the environment as a whole, that is, but how bad can it really be?

The current state of our oceans really is in rapid decline. Humans have a number of impacts on the oceans from destructive fishing practices, oil spills, ocean acidification, disgusting levels of plastic pollution, and more. Some days it is hard for me to grasp how much work there is to be done and how many people there are to reach and inspire to protect the ocean. Despite that, I am hopeful. I've been told I'm an eternal optimist, and when it comes to believing we can reverse the harm we have done and improve ocean health, that is absolutely true. I believe people often do not realize the connection between their daily lives and ocean health, and once they can make that connection they can be inspired to start making small changes that add up to making a big difference. Today, most people only experience a connection with the ocean on their dinner plates. That's why I believe in the power of choosing sustainable seafood. It is an everyday thing most people can do to help the ocean.

What are your thoughts when it comes to wild versus farmed? I always thought wild was the only choice, but I would love to know the differences and the real story.

Not all wild seafood is good and not all farmed seafood is bad. Each have their pros and cons. Some species are more fit than others to withstand fishing pressure. For example, species that are long-lived, reproduce later in life, and have fewer young are vulnerable to overfishing and cannot reproduce at a rate that allows for their populations to be sustainably fished on an industrial scale. However, there are many small species that live shorter lives, reproduce at a young age, and produce abundant offspring that are perfect candidates for sustainable fisheries.

Seafood caught in the wild is caught by a number of different catch methods, many of which can be highly destructive to ocean habitats, or have incidental catches of other, non-targeted species (bycatch), that are usually discarded overboard once they're dead or dying.

Ensuring the fishing heritages continues and that fishing communities are valued, and recognizing the people behind our seafood and their role in bringing food to our tables is important. Not just for posterity's sake, but also in the fight to end human rights abuses in the fishing industry. Seafood is the last wild food we eat; however, our ocean resources alone are not able to sustain a growing global population's appetite for seafood.

Farmed is not an "F" word when it comes to seafood. Farmed seafood provides a resource that supplements wild-caught seafood in a market trying to fulfill the global appetite for seafood. Farmed shellfish (oysters, mussels, and clams) are excellent examples of farmed seafood

that consumers can feel good about buying. There is very little impact on the environment, and, in fact, the filter-feeding shellfish actually clean the water they are grown in and require very little input or energy to grow. However, some farming operations and practices can be detrimental to ocean habitats and wild fish populations. Farms built on sensitive coastal habitats or those that grow large carnivorous fish (tuna ranches and salmon farms, for example) require a lot of feed; feed that usually consists of wild-caught forage fish, which are an important part of the ocean food web. Removing these fish from the wild to feed to farmed fish is robbing other wildlife that depend on these fish for food, and is simply not sustainable. In some cases, it takes over ten times the weight of forage fish to produce one pound of farmed fish. That's like me telling you to give me ten dollars and I will give you a dollar; it simply isn't a good deal (for you, anyway).

In addition to issues with habitat destruction and feed used in farming operations, there are issues of water quality degradation from leftover feed and fish waste. Similar to land-based farming issues from overcrowding of animals, fish farming can lead to an increased occurrence of infections, disease, and parasites, many of which are treated with insecticides and antibiotics that can contaminate surrounding ocean waters.

Innovations are occurring in fish farming to address some of these concerns. For instance, moving fish farms inland and using recirculating water has solved issues of water pollution and risk of escapes of non-native fish to an area. A handful of companies are working to innovate fish feed that reduces or eliminates the amount of wild fish and fish oil used in feed for farmed fish. However, there hasn't been a full solution found to conquer all of the issues, or incentive enough for companies to make the switch from unsustainable farming methods to newer, innovative techniques.

For both wild and farmed seafood there is the aspect of management and regulation by several governmental agencies. Each has their own systems, which can be convoluted and complicated, as is standard in any industry when it comes to government regulation. Pushing local, state, federal, and international governmental bodies to be more responsible and accountable in seafood regulation is important, but ultimately the power rests with the consumer in their buying choices when they demand their seafood comes from sources that are sustainable and well-managed.

What resources are easily available to the retail consumer and what can they do to effect positive change?

The single most effective thing that consumers can do to affect positive change is to be aware that their seafood choices matter to the health of the ocean and that the simple task of asking questions about where and how their seafood is caught or farmed can impact positive change throughout the seafood supply chain. Consumers should ask the following questions:

- What species is this?
- Where was it caught or farmed?
- How was it caught or farmed?
- Is it sustainably sourced?

When consumers use their wallets to vote for seafood that is caught or farmed responsibly and refuse to buy unsustainable options it sends a strong message to chefs, restaurateurs, and grocers that they should also care about how they use their purchasing power to either help or harm the ocean. I have seen firsthand how consumer demand for sustainable seafood has forced positive change on businesses and throughout the seafood supply chain. There is reason to be hopeful.

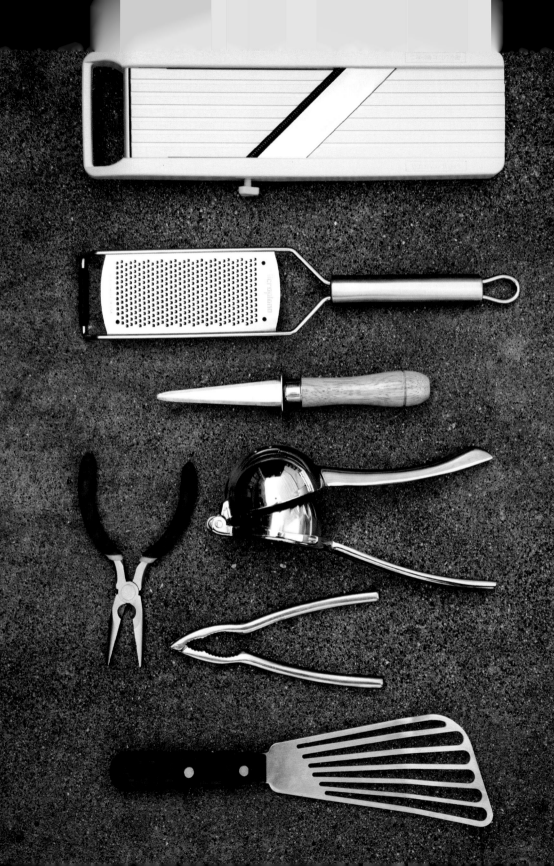

getting started

I sincerely hope this book will be of some value and hopefully encourage many to cook loads of fish, but there are a few things we should do before we get to it. We should identify some equipment and utensils you will hear about in the recipes, some groceries that should also be around, and a couple of items that are handy to keep in the fridge.

Kitchen Equipment and Utensils

- A blender and/or food processor

- Large and small frying pans

- Sauce pot

- Large pot

- Fish spatula

- Citrus zester

- Oyster knife (can double as a clam knife)

- Lobster crackers

- Sharp knives

- Mixing bowls

- Baking trays

- Measuring spoons

- Measuring cups

- Pepper mill

- Digital timer

- Mandolin

- Fish pliers

From the Grocery Store

- Cooking oil (I love safflower oil and rice oil)

- Extra-virgin olive oil

- Champagne vinegar

- White wine vinegar (you can always use champagne vinegar instead)

- Good Dijon mustard (I like Dijon de Maille)

- Kosher Salt

- Whole peppercorns

- Lemons

- Limes

- Butter

- Beer and wine (this is for you, mostly)

Part 2

WINTER

oysters on the half shell
with winter citrus mignonette, basil, and
horseradish / 4

rosé-steamed clams
with leeks, oregano, and
garlic bread / 7

seared day-boat scallops
with mashed cauliflower, apple,
honey-roasted peanuts, and
extra-virgin olive oil / 8

beer-poached mussels
with orzo pasta, olives, prosciutto, and
tarragon / 11

crispy arctic char
with roasted potatoes, escarole,
and chunky fennel, orange, and
basil salsa / 13

whole steamed dungeness crab
with burnt lemon, drawn butter, and
potatoes with bacon / 16

creole gulf prawns
with red beans and rice, shaved celery, and
warm avocado vinaigrette / 19

poached maine lobster
with brussels sprouts, baby carrots, and
mint salsa verde / 21

grilled halibut
with dill potatoes, pistachios,
roasted fennel, and pomegranate
basil sauce / 25

champagne-poached sole
with pickled ginger, tarragon smashed
apples, jasmine rice, and champagne
butter / 26

lemon sole schnitzel
with olive oil crushed potatoes, capers,
lemon, and wild arugula / 29

pan-roasted tru cod
with roasted onions, swiss chard,
winter mushrooms, and kale
pesto / 31

sautéed ling cod
with winter squash bread pudding and red
wine gastrique / 33

smoked haddock tartine
on toasted wheat bread, dill cream cheese,
watercress, and cornichons / 37

smoked salmon and farm egg fritatta
with basil, lemon, chives, and
tomato / 38

yellowfin tuna ceviche
with salted pear, basil, sesame, avocado, and
salt and vinegar potato chips / 41

sautéed wild king salmon
with garlic cucumbers, roasted
endive, and parsley butter sauce / 43

seared yellowfin tuna
with gingery carrots,
tarragon parsnips, and
tangerine vinaigrette / 44

upside down pineapple cake
with lime curd, fresh pineapple,
and basil / 47

a fish tale about winter

the finnish kind of winter

My new colleagues and I left the extremely popular night club and bar, Helmi, at three o'clock in the morning. Needless to say, we were slightly overserved, and being a foreigner and a chef in Finland in the middle of winter, I was completely out of my element. Oddly enough, they had accepted me as their colleague and ultimately their leader. The rite of passage was interesting, though, to say the least. My big surprise began in the wee hours of the morning with a walk across a frozen stretch of the Baltic Sea to a small island, which had a café and sauna. We clinked beer bottles in the sweltering heat of this sauna, and I was under the impression that this was the big surprise—I should have noticed the large hole cut into the ice adjacent to the sauna house.

When it was time to rise to the occasion, we naked-eight strolled along the frozen sea to this same large hole exposing the coldest water on the planet. It felt miles away from the warm sauna hut where my clothes lived. One by one, these crazy Finns leapt in and swam about as if it was noon and they were at Club Med somewhere in the Caribbean. What else was I to do except take the plunge—literally. What a contrast as I felt my heart implode and an unexpected feeling of warmth. I thought I was dying. Then this passed and it was time to get out. I am not Finnish, and was not wired for this lunacy. The real surprise came minutes later when a surge of energy and a total feeling of invigoration took over. This lasted for hours. Perhaps it wasn't lunacy after all.

This celebration, which commenced at three o'clock in the morning, had lasted until eleven o'clock, and we were off to feast. I had envisioned a sort of Viking-warrior-style lunch, but each Finn would remind you that they are not Scandinavians and the Vikings were from Norway. Regardless, when lunch was served, it was magnificent. Thanks to a little insane moment of ice swimming, we were ravenous and alive. At the center of the table was a beautiful arctic char, roasted whole and awaiting its place in our bellies. Dill and butter-poached potatoes, smoked whitefish, pickled herring, roasted beets, butter lettuces, caviars, and mind-blowing sour breads encircled this magnificently roasted cold-water fish. There were marinated cucumbers known as grandma's cucumbers, sausages, wine, and beer. This beat my usual eleven o'clock meal: a sweet and salty meat pastry (the locals know them as lihapiirakka) and a harsh cup of black coffee by the harbor as the fisherman unloaded their boats.

For a usually solemn lot, their faces showed sheer delight. Finns are melancholic by nature, and they discuss this openly. When they dine out, they tend to all order the same thing because notions of individuality, excitement, and even small talk irritate them. But, at this feast they were on fire, and I saw and shared in their admiration and respect for these amazing ingredients. The inherent simplicity and care with how this feast came together would later redefine my cooking. I vowed

to continue this style of cooking when I returned to the States, and I did. Guests in my restaurant are now able to order whole salmon and char, local vegetables, and simple sauces; the flurry of iPhones never fails to supervene and capture the moment.

Winter is a great time to enjoy all sorts of beautiful options from the sea, and it is especially important to support your local fisherman. Fishing in the winter is not only perilous due to weather and sea conditions; the average consumer gravitates toward land animals in these colder months, lessening the demand for seafood and creating additional challenges to the fishing industry.

oysters on the half shell

with winter citrus mignonette, basil, and horseradish

serves 6

2 ounces grapefruit juice

2 ounces lime juice

2 ounces orange juice

1 Tablespoon black pepper, coarsely ground

1 Tablespoon raw shallots, minced

1 teaspoon thyme leaves, destemmed

1 Tablespoon basil leaves, sliced

1 teaspoon fresh horseradish, grated

18 oysters of your choice

Lemon wedges, for garnish

what to drink

- Melon de Bourgogne
- Champagne
- Lager-style beer
- Gin and sparkling lemonade served over ice

what to ask the fish guy

Ask when the oysters were harvested. By law, they must keep shellfish tags on hand, so they should be able to assist. If the harvest date is more than five days ago, don't buy them. This doesn't mean they are necessarily bad, but the quality may be lesser. Unless you are visiting an oyster farm in Marshall, California, the likelihood of getting same-day oysters is slim. Up to four days is normally fine.

method

Combine all ingredients except the oysters and lemon wedges and let them sit for at least 30 minutes—this is your mignonette. Wash the oysters while the mignonette is steeping, a process which allows the flavors to marry perfectly and soften the shallots. Many hardware stores and grocery stores carry "nail brushes." They double nicely as an oyster scrubber, but any medium to firm bristle-scrubbing brush will suffice. Under running cold water, scrub the oysters individually, focusing on the seam where the two shells meet. It doesn't need to be perfect, as a little sand won't hurt you.

When the oysters are washed and scrubbed, it's time to shuck. Please keep in mind the minimum resting time for the mignonette. It is best to refrigerate the cleaned oysters and allow for the mignonette to be ready. Use a kitchen towel to hold the oyster in place, and find the joint or small opening at the thickest end of the oyster where the two shells meet. Place the larger side of the oyster on a table, still using a towel to protect your hand and allow for a firm grip. Gently place the tip of an oyster knife into this joint. Wiggle it in until it clearly stops, and press down on the oyster to pop the top shell open (similar to opening a can of paint). Once it pops open, use the oyster knife to scrape it along the inside surface of the shell to cut the oyster away from the shell. Try not to lose any of the liquid—it is delicious! It is always best to serve them on ice so they remain cold, and the mignonette should be served on the side with a small spoon so that people can take as much or as little as they wish. That's it!

plating

On any plate, a linen, some lettuce, or a towel can be set first to help the ice and ultimately the oysters from sliding off the plate. Crush some ice and fill the plate generously. Set the oyster shells down on top of the ice, and serve the mignonette on the side. It's usually a good idea to have lemon wedges available as well.

rosé-steamed clams

with leeks, oregano, and garlic bread

---

serves 4

1 really good baguette

2 cloves garlic, chopped, center
   removed

1 cup melted butter

1 cup parsley leaves, sliced

1 pound manila clams

1 ounce preferred cooking oil

1 large leek, chopped

1 shallot, peeled, chopped

1 Tablespoon whole, unsalted butter

1 pinch salt

2 cups delicious rosé wine (I like to
   use the wines of Provence)

½ teaspoon ground pepper

1 Tablespoon lemon juice

1 Tablespoon fresh oregano leaves

---

what to drink

- The obvious—the same wine you
  used to cook this
- Wheat beer
- For the cocktail: a pisco sour

what to ask the fish guy

With all shellfish, my first question is "when was this harvested"? I usually give them a reasonable max of five days—if older than that, don't buy them.

method

Preheat your oven to 350°F. Slice the baguette in half, lengthwise, and then slice it horizontally, as though you are about to make two very big sandwiches—which you are not. Add the chopped garlic to the melted butter and let it simmer in a small pot or pan on a low temperature for 5 minutes. Line up the four baguette sections on a sheet tray with the cut side facing up. Add the parsley leaves to the melted butter mixture, then, using a pastry brush, generously brush the inside sides of the four baguette pieces. Make sure you are scooping the garlic pieces and parsley so they get evenly spread on the baguette. Bake in the oven for 10 minutes or until golden brown. Please check the bread regularly. When it's ready, let it rest at room temperature and begin cooking the clams.

Place clams in a bowl of cold water. Let them sit for 10 minutes, then move them around to remove any sand that may still be present. Heat the cooking oil in a pot. When you see it about to smoke, add the leeks and shallots. Immediately remove the pan from the heat and add the butter. Add the pinch of salt, and stir the ingredients in the pot. Return the pan to the heat, keeping it on a medium heat, and continue to stir until the leeks and shallots are translucent. Add the clams to the pot and stir for 30 seconds. Pour the wine into the pot and keep on a medium heat. This next part is critical. You must stand over the pot and watch as the clams begin to open. The moment they open is when they must be removed from the pot. Have a separate bowl, ultimately the serving bowl, close by to pluck them from the pot and place in this bowl. You will have the occasional clam that doesn't open. Throw those guys away. Once the clams are out of the pot and in the bowl, add the pepper, lemon juice, and oregano leaves to the cooking liquid. Next, pour this over the clams and serve with the garlic bread on the side. I really love using this to sop up the leftover clam broth.

plating

You already have the serving bowl next to the pot of clams, so you're halfway there. In preparing the table, it's a good idea to have a bowl for each person and one extra for the discarded shells. Small forks are handy for digging the clams from the shell, and spoons for eating the broth like soup. The clams should be piled up, but that's your call. No real need to be overly pedantic here. Then, there's the bread. You can tear it, cut it into pieces, or leave it in sections and chomp on it. This is up to you.

seared day-boat scallops

with mashed cauliflower, apple, honey-roasted peanuts, and extra-virgin olive oil

serves 4

1 medium-sized head of cauliflower

Salt and pepper, as desired

2 Tablespoons extra-virgin olive oil

1 Tablespoon lemon juice

2 Granny Smith apples, core removed, peeled, and ribboned

12 U/10 day-boat scallops

1 Tablespoon mint leaves, thinly sliced

½ cup honey-roasted peanuts, for garnish

what to drink

- A yeasty champagne. Something along the lines of Tattinger or Jacquesson
- White wines from Burgundy Puligny Montrachet, for example
- In the world of beers, a Belgian triple would be great
- Pisco sour

what to ask the fish guy

First, ask if they will clean them for you—in the US, scallops usually make it to market already cleaned, as many parts outside the obvious meat are not the most beautiful; many are quite delicious though, such as the roe. Next, ask if the scallops are previously frozen. It's not the end of the world if they are, but it makes cooking them a bit more challenging. You want fresh day-boat scallops. If they are from the northeast Atlantic seaboard, you found the best.

method

Cut the head of cauliflower in half, lengthwise; it is easier to see where the florets meet the inner stem. Cut each floret off and try to keep them close in size; this way they will cook evenly. Set a small pot of water to boil, and add the cauliflower and a pinch of salt. Cook the cauliflower until soft, roughly 6 to 8 minutes. Drain the water and allow the cauliflower to remain in the pot. Using a wooden spoon, mash the cauliflower into a lumpy mashed potato-like substance. Mix in 1 tablespoon of the olive oil, the lemon juice, and salt and pepper, as desired. Fold in the apples, and set aside.

Season the scallops lightly with a gentle sprinkle of salt. Heat a sauté or frying pan on high with enough oil to coat the bottom of the pan. When the oil begins to smoke, add the seasoned scallops and turn the heat down to medium. Move the scallops around in the pan, keeping the side with which you began still cooking in the oil. Cook until that side is golden brown, and turn the scallops over onto the opposite side; this is usually 2 minutes. Once flipped, turn the heat back up to high and repeat the process for about 1 minute. This should take no longer than 3 to 4 minutes, and the scallops should be soft and still a bit raw inside. Remove the scallops from the pan onto a plate. Reheat the cauliflower and apple mixture gently, and fold in the mint leaves.

plating

Place a spoonful of the apple and cauliflower mixture on the plate, and set the scallops on top. Sprinkle the honey-roasted peanuts on and around the set, and drizzle a small amount of that good olive oil around the plate, as well.

beer-poached mussels

with orzo pasta, olives, prosciutto, and tarragon

serves 4

½ cup dry orzo pasta

1 Tablespoon extra-virgin olive oil

8 thin slices prosciutto

2 fluid ounces cooking oil

2 whole shallots, peeled, sliced

2 fluid ounces white cooking wine
(should still be drinkable)

2 pounds fresh mussels

2 (12-ounce) bottles lager beer
(Anchor Lager from Anchor
Brewing is my first choice)

1 teaspoon fresh thyme leaves

¼ cup Cerignola olives or your
favorite green olives, pitted, sliced

1 teaspoon fresh tarragon leaves,
sliced

Juice of 1 lemon

Zest of 1 lemon

Salt and pepper, as desired

what to drink

- Belgian white ale
- Rosé from Provence
- Greyhound

what to ask the fish guy

Ask for PEI (Prince Edward Island) Mussels. To be honest, I lived with a few Canadians once upon a time, and I found them uncomfortably kind and annoyingly more organized, politically—but their mussels are the best. If you have willing fishmongers in front of you, ask if they are willing to debeard the mussels for you. The stringy little hairs that peek out of the mussel are inedible and referred to as the beard (technically, byssal threads, which allow them to attach to their surroundings). If the fishmongers won't debeard them for you, ask them then to show you how. You need to wash each mussel, as they can be sandy, and then you need to grab those little fibers peeking out and gently wiggle them out.

method

Preheat your oven to 350°F. Set a pot of water on the stove to boil, and place the orzo in. Cook for 8 to 9 minutes or until your preferred doneness. Pour this through a strainer, run under cold water until it is at or below room temperature, and toss with extra-virgin olive oil. Place this aside for a few minutes. Place prosciutto slices on a baking pan lined with parchment or wax paper. Bake for 8 minutes and remove from the oven. It should resemble bacon and be a bit crispy without burning or tasting bitter.

In a small pot, add enough cooking oil to just cover the bottom and place over medium-high heat. As the oil is just about to smoke, add your sliced shallots and lower the heat to medium. After 5 minutes, add the white wine and cook until the pot is almost dry. Add the cleaned mussels (see below in "what to ask the fish guy") to your shallot mixture, then add the beer and thyme leaves. (Save yourself a sip, it's called quality control.) Turn the heat to high and stand there and watch as the mussels open. I'm a big believer in the notion of simply standing by any shellfish while steaming and pulling them out of the liquid one by one as they open. If they don't open, your best bet is to toss them, so keep a bowl handy to place the opened mussels as they pop! Once the open mussels are all in the bowl, add the orzo, olives, olive oil, and tarragon to the leftover mussel broth and lower the temperature to a simmer.

Using a dessert or coffee spoon, scoop the cooked mussels out of the shell and, once all out of the shell, add to the pot of cooking liquid. At this point, add in the cooked orzo and all other ingredients. Add the lemon juice, zest, and salt and pepper, as desired.

Continued on page 12

Serve the pot as a dish to share. Grab a ladle and some bowls and have at it. I recommend keeping the prosciutto separate. Crumbling it in at the last moment or eating it as a chip throughout both work very well. As the mussel shells should be discarded at this point, this is a pretty easy one. It works like a minestrone, but if you have some extra olives or tarragon leaves, go ahead and add them if your palate wants a more assertive flavor profile.

crispy arctic char

with roasted potatoes, escarole, and chunky fennel, orange, and basil salsa

---

serves 4

6 fluid ounces cooking oil

1 fennel bulb with top, chopped into medium, equal-sized pieces (reserve fronds for garnish)

½ cup red onion, minced

½ cup white wine

1 cup whole parsley leaves, destemmed

1 cup basil leaves, destemmed, torn into pieces

½ cup extra-virgin olive oil

Zest of 1 orange

Juice of 1 orange

Salt and pepper, as desired

1 pound small potatoes, cut into wedges

2 heads of escarole, darker exterior leaves discarded, well-rinsed, set to dry

4 (5–6-ounce) arctic char filets, skin on, pin bones removed

juice of 1 lemon

zest of 1 lemon

what to drink

- Chenin blanc
- Vinho verde
- Pilsner beer
- Botanical gin gimlet

what to ask the fish guy

Ask for 4 (5–6-ounce) portions, skin on, scaled, and pin bones removed. This will leave you with a ready to go, portioned fish. When setting up the kitchen, check for those little pin bones again. They can be gently pulled out with needle nose pliers if the fishmonger missed one.

method

Set a frying pan over medium–high heat and add enough cooking oil to coat the bottom of the pan. Once it begins to smoke, add the fennel and red onions. Lower the heat, and stir regularly. Cook for 2 to 3 minutes, and add the white wine. Continue cooking for 2 more minutes or until the pan is almost dry, and transfer the contents to a food processor or blender. Add the parsley, basil, olive oil, orange zest, orange juice, and a pinch of salt and pepper. Mix this for a few seconds and stop. Scrape the sides of the bowl, and mix again for only a few seconds. Set this aside for plating.

Set a frying pan over medium heat, and coat the bottom of the pan with cooking oil. When it is about to smoke, add the potatoes, and turn the heat to low. Cook for 5 minutes and turn them over; they should be golden brown. Cook the other side for 5 minutes or until the potatoes are soft in the center. Turn the heat to high, wait 10 seconds, and add the escarole leaves. Cook for 30 seconds, add the lemon zest, lemon juice, and a pinch of salt and pepper. Set this aside for plating, and let's cook this fish!

Preheat a large skillet over a medium heat; if you don't have one, you can use a large frying pan.

Season the char gently, lightly, and evenly with salt and pepper. Pat the skin dry with a paper towel. Add a small amount of cooking oil to the skillet, and when you see it slightly smoke,

Continued on page 14

place the fish in the oil, skin side down. Increase the heat for one minute and then return it to medium. After 1 minute, using a spatula, gently lift the fish from the oil, ensuring that it is not sticking. Once it is able to move about the pan, lower the heat to medium-low, and watch as the filet is cooked through the skin. When it appears that the filet is only slightly raw, turn it over and sear the other side for 10 seconds.

plating

Set the escarole and potatoes in the center of the plate, and place the piece of cooked char on top. Spoon the chunky salsa around this set, and scatter fennel fronds about for garnish. If your fennel already had the tops cut off, you could use dill or just omit it.

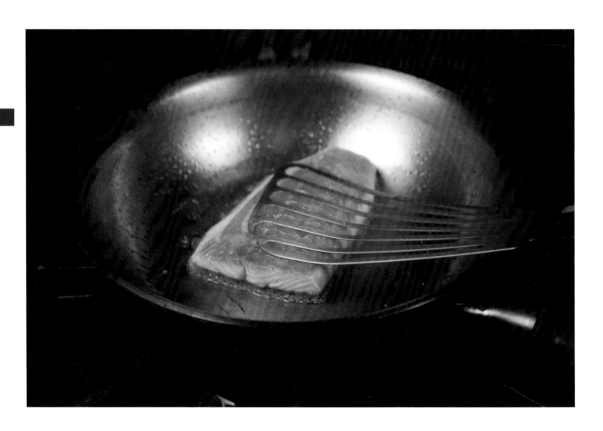

whole steamed dungeness crab

with burnt lemon, drawn butter, and potatoes with bacon

serves 4

1 pound fingerling potatoes,
    halved lengthwise

Salt and pepper, as desired

1 teaspoon Dijon mustard

1 Tablespoon extra-virgin olive oil

1 Tablespoon white wine vinegar

4 strips bacon, cooked to desired
    crispiness, roughly chopped

1 Tablespoon fresh parsley leaves,
    sliced

½ pound lightly salted butter

2 lemons, quartered lengthwise

2 (2-pound) whole crabs

Lobster crackers, for garnish

what to drink

- Your favorite beer
- Blanc de blanc champagne
- Rum punch

what to ask the fish guy

These guys can usually steam and crack the crab into sections for you. Let them. It's a messy business to do it yourself, but if you are up for it, you will need a pot of boiling water and another big bowl of ice water, enough to fit two crabs. If each crab is 2 pounds each and they are steamed in a rolling boil, they'll need to cook for 10 minutes.

If you want to serve them warm, you don't need to shove them into the ice water after the ten minutes is up. I prefer them cold, so the ice water ensures a perfectly cold product. Again, if the fish guys will steam the crab for you, go for it, and let them crack and clean them, as well.

method

Place potatoes and a pinch of salt in a small pot of cold water, and bring up to a simmer. Check them periodically, as the cooking time will vary, but they should be cooked through and fork tender after 10 minutes of simmering. Once they are fork-tender, pour out excess water and leave in pot. Add the mustard, olive oil, vinegar, bacon, parsley, and your preferred amount of salt and pepper. Set this aside for later. Place the butter in a separate pot and set over a low heat. The idea here is to slowly melt it, not to cook it.

Now, we are going to burn lemons, but we are not going to set them on fire—regardless of how much fun that sounds. As they are cut in quarters, you have options. If you have a torch, torch them only on the cut side and not on the skin side; you just want to char them a bit, not fully blacken them. This is the fastest way. The next choice is a grill. The idea is the same; grill just the fleshy side of the lemons until charred. Lastly, and it still works, is to do this with a hot pan over your kitchen stove's burner; no oil needed, just sear them in the dry pan. Once charred, set them aside.

For the crab, refer to the section below, as this is something the fish guy should be able to do for you. We will get into that later. Once the crab is ready, make sure everyone has lobster crackers, heat the potato mixture, and make sure the butter is warm. This is getting exciting!

plating

Once the crab is ready, whether you are serving warm or cold, set on a platter with the lemons, warm drawn butter, and potatoes with bacon. Have a bowl to discard shells and shellfish/lobster crackers; this can get messy, so some moist towels are a nice touch. I love to dunk the crab in the butter, return to my plate, discard the shells, and squeeze the lemon on top. Tough to argue this one.

creole gulf prawns

with red beans and rice, shaved celery, and warm avocado vinaigrette

---

serves 6

red beans and rice

3 cups canned, organic kidney beans
  or 2 cups dry kidney beans

½ teaspoon prepared creole
  seasoning

1 Tablespoon fresh oregano leaves

2 Tablespoons unsalted butter,
  softened

1 Tablespoon lime juice

Salt and pepper, as desired

2 cups long-grain white rice

avocado vinaigrette

1 ripe avocado, peeled, core removed

2 Tablespoons lime juice

3 Tablespoons extra-virgin olive oil

1 Tablespoon red onion, minced

1 Tablespoon cilantro leaves, sliced

1 Tablespoon parsley leaves, sliced

Salt and pepper, as desired

prawns

2½ pounds wild gulf prawns, peeled,
  deveined

½ teaspoon prepared creole
  seasoning

Salt, as desired

Extra-virgin olive oil, as desired

½ cup your favorite white wine

2 stalks celery, ribboned, for garnish

what to drink

- Pilsner-style beer
- Oregon Pinot Noir
- German Riesling
- Rye old-fashioned

what to ask the fish guy

Make sure you are buying wild gulf prawns from the Gulf of Mexico, preferably skim-net caught. Buy the peeled and deveined product. I love the 16/20 sizing. If you can find it, the U/9's are great (this means that less than 9 make up one pound). Avoid the farm-raised product from Asia. The methods are questionable and flavor is not nearly as delicious.

method: red beans and rice

If you bought the cooked, organic kidney beans, rinse them well. If you went the dry route, set a pot with at least 5 cups of water and the 2 cups of beans on the stove; do not add salt. And, no, you do not need to soak the beans if you follow this method. Bring the beans to a boil for 5 minutes, and then shut off the heat. Let them sit for 30 minutes, and then return them to the heat. Cook them over a low to medium heat, stirring regularly and adding water as needed, as they will dry out. When the beans are soft and slightly creamy, add the creole seasoning, oregano leaves, softened butter, lime juice, salt and pepper as desired. Leave it on the stove, heat off, for later. In a separate pot, bring 6 cups of water and a pinch of salt to a boil. Add the rice and stir. Check regularly to make sure it's tender. After 8 minutes, it should be done. Strain and rinse until it is cool. Now, add the rice to the beans and gently fold them together. Taste this and decide if you want more salt, creole seasoning, or lime juice.

method: avocado vinaigrette

Mash the avocado in a bowl. Add lime juice, olive oil, red onion, cilantro, parsley, and salt and pepper, as you prefer. Whisk it well in the same bowl and place in a small pot. Warm it gently and reserve for later.

19

Continued on page 20

method: prawns

Generously season the prawns with the creole seasoning. Gently sprinkle a small amount of salt and refrigerate until you are ready to cook them. In a large sauté pan or skillet, heat enough oil to coat the bottom of the pan. Set on high heat, and when the oil begins to slightly smoke, add the seasoned prawns. Spread them evenly, and allow the first side to sear. Turn the little guys over after 2 minutes and let the other side sear. After 1 minute, add the white wine and cook until the pan is dry. Turn the heat off, and gently reheat the red beans and rice. Let's get to plating.

plating

Place a large spoonful of the beans and rice on the plate. Place the prawns atop the beans and rice. Add in the celery ribbons however you see fit. Drizzle a bit of the avocado vinaigrette on the prawns and around the plate. Now, serve!

poached maine lobster

with brussels sprouts, baby carrots, and mint salsa verde

---

serves 4

lobster with brussels sprouts and baby carrots

1 Tablespoon salt

1 pound Brussels sprouts, quartered lengthwise

2 ounces neutral cooking oil

1 pound baby carrots, peeled

Salt and pepper, as desired

2 (1½-pound) live Maine lobsters

mint salsa verde

1 cup mint leaves

1 cup parsley leaves

1 cup extra-virgin olive oil

Salt and pepper, as desired

½ cup basil leaves

1 bunch chives, diced

Juice of 2 lemons

Zest of 2 lemons

1 Tablespoon diced red onions

2 ounces white wine vinegar

---

what to drink

- White burgundy
- Pinot blanc
- An IPA
- Botanical gin on the rocks topped off with sparkling lemonade

what to ask the fish guy

Ask if the lobsters are from Maine or at least the same New England coast. They are the best. If they only have spiny lobsters, that's okay too, but don't expect any claws. If they are willing to steam them for you, do it; it's a lot less hassle and mess. Just remember to tell them you will warm them up later, so a lighter steaming is preferred.

method: lobster with brussels sprouts and baby carrots

Preheat your oven to 400°F. Fill a large bowl with ice and water. Place two large pots of water on the stove and bring to a boil; add salt to one of them until you can just taste it, and do not add salt to the other. Boil the Brussels sprouts in the salted water until they are slightly tender, not cooked through, 2 to 3 minutes. Move them to the bowl of ice water and cool rapidly. Remove from the ice and set aside for later. Keep the ice water. In a baking pan, heat the cooking oil and add the baby carrots. Keep them moving around the pan to cook them evenly. Once they are tender, add the Brussels sprouts and cook until they are tender. Season as desired with salt and pepper, and keep at room temperature.

Let's cook the lobsters. Have a large pair of tongs and a large spoon ready. Look at the lobsters and make sure the rubber bands are still around their claws—it can be very interesting if not! Place them quickly into the unsalted boiling water and use the tongs and spoon to dunk them. Keep a safe distance as they may flap their tail and splash some hot water on you. Set your timer for 8 minutes. When the 8 minutes are up, move the lobsters to the ice water. Let them sit there for a few minutes; enough time to make the salsa verde.

Remove the lobsters from the ice water and place on a cutting board. Pull off the claws and tails. Crack the claws. Split the tails down the middle, shell on, but be very careful, as the tail can slip. Place all the lobster parts in the pan with the Brussels sprouts and carrots, and return the pan to the oven. Let cook for 5 minutes or enough to gently warm the lobster through. Use a timer here, as well; overcooking lobster results in a chewy and pointless eating experience.

21

Continued on page 22

method: mint salsa verde

In a blender, add the mint, parsley, and olive oil and purée. Then, add a pinch of salt and pepper, basil, chives, lemon juice, lemon zest, red onions, and vinegar. Purée again to desired consistency, and adjust seasoning with salt, pepper, and lemon juice, as desired.

plating

While the lobster is in the oven, pour the seasoned and ready-to-serve salsa verde into small bowl so that people can take as much as they wish. Remove the pan and arrange its contents on a large plate or platter. This one works well as a buffet item or served family style.

grilled halibut

with dill potatoes, pistachios, roasted fennel, and pomegranate basil sauce

---

serves 4

pomegranate basil sauce

1 pomegranate, seeds removed

1 cup fresh basil leaves

1 Tablespoon aged balsamic vinegar

1 teaspoon lime juice

1 Tablespoon cracked black pepper

1 teaspoon salt

1 teaspoon ground coriander

grilled halibut with dill potatoes, pistachios, and roasted fennel

2 fennel bulbs, tops removed, cut into ¼-inch sections lengthwise

1 pinch of salt

2 Tablespoons neutral cooking oil

1 pound small potatoes, washed very well, poked with a fork

4 (5-ounce) halibut filets, skin-off

1 cup wild arugula

1 cup salted and roasted pistachios, shelled

---

what to drink

- Riesling from the Alsace region
- Oregon Pinot Noir
- Flemish red ale
- Bourbon old-fashioned

what to ask the fish guy

Ask for Alaskan Halibut; it is the most sustainable and yields the highest amount. Have her or him cut you 5-ounce portions, and ask for the skin to be removed.

method: pomegranate basil sauce

In a blender, mix pomegranate seeds, basil leaves, balsamic vinegar, lime juice, black pepper, salt, and coriander. Blend for 2–3 minutes, and adjust seasoning with salt and pepper as desired. Reserve for later.

method: grilled halibut with dill potatoes, pistachios, and roasted fennel

Preheat your oven to 400°F. Toss fennel in cooking oil and season with a pinch of salt. Lay fennel on a baking tray and place in oven. Cook for 10 minutes and turn over. Cook for another 5 minutes and, using a small knife, test for tenderness. Continue cooking until tender and remove from oven. Remove from the tray, and let sit at room temperature until later. Add potatoes to the same tray and cook until tender. Add to roasted fennel and reserve until later.

Fire up the grill. (Make sure it's cleaned very well and oiled generously.) Drizzle oil generously over the fish, and lightly season with salt and pepper. Grill the halibut, moving it regularly to create an even charring. Grill on one side for 5 minutes, and turn over using a fish spatula or small metal spatula. Cook for another 3 to 4 minutes on the turned side, checking regularly for doneness. Cooking halibut slightly undercooked is the best, as it can be eaten raw. If cooked to medium, it retains its moisture and optimal flavor. Pop the fennel and potatoes in the oven and quickly reheat. Now, let's plate this!

plating

Place a small handful of arugula on the plate, and top with the roasted fennel and potatoes. Sprinkle some pistachios on this mix. Place cooked halibut on top of the vegetable garnish, and drizzle the pomegranate sauce around the fish, as desired. Serve immediately.

champagne-poached sole

with pickled ginger, tarragon smashed apples, jasmine rice, and champagne butter

serves 4

¾ cup jasmine rice

Salt and pepper, as desired

1 bottle champagne or sparkling wine

2 whole shallots, peeled, roughly chopped

juice of 4 limes

2 Tablespoons pickled ginger liquid

2 Granny Smith apples, peeled, cores removed

1 Tablespoon fresh tarragon leaves, diced

Juice of 1 lemon

Zest of 1 lemon

½ cup pickled ginger

Zest of 4 limes

4 (5–6-ounce) sole filets

½ pound unsalted butter, diced, chilled

1 Tablespoon Dijon mustard

1 teaspoon fresh thyme leaves

what to drink

- Champagne; unless you were sipping throughout the cooking process, which I recommend, you should still have some left
- Pinot gris
- Kölsch
- Pisco sour

what to ask the fish guy

Ask for the best and freshest filets of sole without the skin. If the sizing is too small, you may need two filets around 2 to 3 ounces each per person. If sole is unavailable, you can substitute most of the flat fishes. If you end up with halibut, allow it to simmer 7 to 8 minutes.

method

Rinse the rice well in cold running water. Then, add the rice to a sauce pot with 3 cups of cold water and a pinch of salt. Bring to a boil, uncovered, and then reduce to a simmer. Stir occasionally, and cook for 10 to 12 minutes or until tender. Rinse under cold running water and reserve for later. In a shallow pan, one with sides, simmer half of the champagne, chopped shallots, lime juice, and pickled ginger liquid for 15 minutes. This is your poaching liquid. Place on very low heat.

Combine the peeled apples, tarragon, and lemon juice and zest in a mixing bowl. Using a wooden spoon, smash into small pieces. Reserve this for later. Set a pan on the stove, and add 1 ounce of poaching liquid to the pan. Add in the rice, tarragon smashed apple mixture, pickled ginger, and lime zest and season as desired. Reserve this for later. Bring the poaching liquid up to a simmer and add the sole filets. Let them cook for 3 to 4 minutes and remove from the liquid. Take 6 fluid ounces of the poaching liquid and place in a pan, discarding the rest. Add the mustard and thyme leaves and a pinch of salt. Whisk well and add the butter in little by little, whisking rapidly. Once the sauce is smooth, adjust seasoning with salt and pepper.

plating

Place the rice, ginger, and tarragon smashed apple mixture on the plate, and place the sole filet on top. Pour the sauce generously over the top and serve immediately.

lemon sole schnitzel

with olive oil crushed potatoes, capers, lemon, and wild arugula

serves 4

1 pound fingerling potatoes, washed, cut into equal-sized pieces

Salt and pepper, as desired

juice of 1 lemon

zest of 1 lemon

2 Tablespoons capers, well-rinsed

2 Tablespoons parsley leaves, roughly chopped

3 Tablespoons extra-virgin olive oil

4 (5–6-ounce) sole filets

1 cup all-purpose flour

3 eggs, whisked

3 cups panko bread crumbs

4 fluid ounces of cooking oil

1 pound wild arugula, well-rinsed, destemmed (it often comes this way by the bag)

1 lemon, cut into wedges

what to drink

- Grüner Veltliner
- Pinot grigio
- Hefeweizen
- Salty dog cocktail

what to ask the fish guy

Ask for the best and freshest filets of sole without the skin. If the sizing is too small, you may need 2 filets, around 2 to 3 ounces each per person. If sole is unavailable, you can substitute most of the flat fishes. If you end up with halibut, you will need to gently pound the filets with a meat mallet, but a better way would be to ask for four extremely thinly sliced pieces.

method

In a medium pot, bring the cut potatoes to a boil, beginning with cold water and a pinch of salt, and then lower to a simmer. Once they are very tender and cooked all the way through, drain the water. Season potatoes with another pinch of salt and pepper, and then add the lemon juice, zest, capers, parsley, and olive oil. Mix together with a spoon and reserve it for later in the same pot.

Prepare the fish for pan frying by placing them on a baking tray or bowl with flour. Cover them evenly, and then gently pat them to remove all excess flour. Place the fish in the whisked eggs, and then into a pan or bowl with the bread crumbs. Once evenly coated with the bread crumbs, place on a plate and refrigerate.

Set a large frying pan on the stove and cover the bottom of the pan with the cooking oil. Heat until the oil begins to just start smoking, and add the breaded filets to the oil. Turn the heat up a bit to allow the oil to recover, and monitor closely. The fish need 3 to 4 minutes and will be ready. They will be golden brown and slightly firm to the touch. Remove from the heat and place on a plate covered in paper towels, a paper shopping bag, or something to absorb the oil. Season the fish lightly with salt. Heat the potato mixture and have the wild arugula ready. Off to plating!

plating

Set a large spoonful of potatoes next to a handful of arugula. Place the fish on top of this, and garnish with lemon wedges; often a squeeze of fresh lemon is lovely with this preparation.

pan-roasted tru cod

with roasted onions, swiss chard, winter mushrooms, and kale pesto

serves 4

2 medium yellow onions, peeled, quartered lengthwise

Salt and pepper, as desired

2 cups baby kale leaves, firmly packed

1 cup extra-virgin olive oil

Juice of 2 lemons

Zest of 2 lemons

2 cloves of garlic, peeled, boiled for 4 minutes

2 Tablespoons sherry vinegar

¼ cup pine nuts, lightly toasted

½ cup freshly grated Parmesan cheese

Neutral cooking oil, as desired

½ pound winter mushrooms (black trumpet, hedgehog, and yellowfoot are great, but maitake and cremini which are available all year are fine substitutions)

1 shallot, peeled, thinly sliced

1 bunch green Swiss chard leaves, destemmed

4 (5-ounce) Pacific tru cod filets, skin on

1 teaspoon unsalted butter

what to drink

- Rose champagne
- Verdicchio (Italian white wine)
- Belgian-style golden ale
- Botanical gin martini

what to ask the fish guy

Ask for the thicker side of the Alaskan Tru Cod loin, and let them know you want the portions to be 5 ounces each. Although it might sound like you are asking a lot, ask them to leave the skin on and slightly score the skin down the middle. This shouldn't be a problem as they have the knives and they are cutting this for you anyway. By scoring the skin, the fish will cook more evenly as the skin will stay in the cooking oil throughout the process. If not, there is a good possibility that the fish will buckle or curve away from the oil, leaving the center uncooked.

method

Preheat oven to 375°F. Toss the quartered onions with oil, salt and pepper, place on a baking sheet, and place in preheated oven. These will roast for approximately 30 minutes, but check them every 5 minutes to see if they are golden brown and tender. While the onions are roasting, make the pesto. In a blender, add the kale, olive oil, lemon juice and zest, boiled garlic cloves, sherry vinegar, pine nuts, and Parmesan. Blend to desired consistency and season as you wish with salt and pepper. Reserve for later. And check those onions!

Set a frying pan on the stove, add just enough cooking oil to cover the bottom of the pan, and wait until it just starts smoking. Add the mushrooms to the pan, and lower the heat to medium. Move the mushrooms around in the pan, cooking evenly for 3 to 4 minutes. Now, add the sliced shallots and set the heat on low. Cook the shallots for 3 minutes and then add the Swiss chard leaves. Increase the heat to high, cook for 1 minute, and remove from heat. Add a pinch of salt and pepper. The onions should be golden brown and tender by now. Remove them from the oven and set aside. Everything else is ready, so the last step is the fish.

In a medium-sized frying pan, heat enough oil to just cover the base of the pan and set over high heat. Pat the skin of the cod dry with a paper towel, and season with an even sprinkling of salt and pepper. The patting-dry step will prevent the fish from sticking to the pan. Once the oil in the pan begins to

31

Continued on page 32

smoke, place the fish gently in the pan with the skin side down. Let the fish cook for 30 seconds and lower the heat to medium. Cook them for 1 minute, and using a fish spatula or a thin metal spatula, lift the fish and move it slightly to ensure the skin is not sticking to the pan. Add the teaspoon of butter to the pan and cook for 2 more minutes. Turn the cod over onto the opposite side, and cook for 3 to 4 minutes. Check them every 30 seconds and cook until the fish is firm; if you want to peek inside, do it! The fish should be opaque and set firmly. Serve immediately.

plating

Place the mushrooms and chard in the center of the plate, and then place a piece of roasted onion alongside. Generously spoon the kale pesto around this garnish. Place the fish on top and you're all set!

sautéed ling cod

with winter squash bread pudding and red wine gastrique

---

serves 6

bread pudding

2 Tablespoons cooking oil

3 cups butternut squash, peeled, seeds removed, chopped into medium-sized pieces

Juice of 2 limes

1 Tablespoon cinnamon

Salt and pepper, as desired

6 eggs

3 cups whole milk

1 cup heavy whipping cream

Zest of 2 limes

1 cup fresh sage leaves, chopped

1 cup fresh parsley leaves, chopped

1 (1-pound) loaf of sourdough bread, cubed, toasted

2 Tablespoons whole butter

red wine gastrique

1 bottle inexpensive red wine

2 Tablespoons granulated sugar

1 whole shallot, peeled, sliced

½ cup red wine vinegar

1 Teaspoon cracked black pepper

1 pinch salt

1 Tablespoon fresh thyme leaves

cod

Neutral cooking oil, as desired

6 (5-ounce) portions of Ling Cod

Salt and pepper, as desired

1 teaspoon butter

1 bunch watercress or wild arugula, for garnish

what to drink

- A light red Burgundy such as Chambolle-Musigny
- A Mendocino County or Anderson Valley California Pinot Noir
- Red ale
- Old-fashioned

what to ask the fish guy

Ask for the thicker side of the cod loin and let them know you want the portions to be 5 ounces each. Although it might sound like you are asking a lot, ask them to leave the skin on and slightly score the skin down the middle; this shouldn't be a problem, as they are already cutting the fish for you anyway. By scoring the skin, it will stay in the cooking oil throughout the process and cook more evenly. If the skin is not scored, there is a good possibility that the fish will buckle, or curve away from the oil, leaving the center uncooked.

method: bread pudding

Preheat oven to 325°F. Heat a large frying pan and coat the bottom with the cooking oil. When it begins to smoke, add the cubed squash and turn the heat to low. Move the pieces around in the pan using a wooden spoon to evenly color and cook the squash. Once they are tender, add the lime juice, cinnamon, and a pinch of salt and pepper. Allow this to cool.

In a mixing bowl, whisk together the eggs, milk, cream, lime zest, sage, and parsley. Once it is mixed completely, fold in the toasted bread and pan-roasted squash. Let this sit for 10 minutes. Using the whole butter, generously grease a 9 x 9 x 2-inch baking pan or small loaf pan with butter. Using a large spoon, spoon the mixture into the pan, and pour in any excess liquid from the bowl. Place the pan in the preheated oven. This will take between 45 minutes to 1 hour. You will know when it is ready, as it will be spongy and no longer a liquid consistency. Cover the bread pudding with foil after 30 minutes have passed; this will prevent it from getting too dark. Now, set the timer for 15 minutes. If it isn't ready after that, check it every few

Continued on page 34

minutes. Once it has set and feels like a spongy cake, remove it from the oven, remove the foil, and let it cool in the pan.

method: red wine gastrique

Open the wine and have a taste; you've already earned it. In a small saucepan, add the sugar and place over medium heat. Stand there and watch as it slowly liquefies. It will soon begin to turn brown; this is when you need to move quickly. Add the sliced shallots to the light brown sugar and cook for 30 seconds. Then, add the vinegar and cracked black pepper. Simmer this until the pan is almost dry, approximately 4 to 5 minutes. Then, add the remaining red wine. Simmer this for 30 to 40 minutes or until it is syrup-like in consistency. Regularly use a small spoon to test its thickness. Once it is ready, add a pinch of salt and the thyme leaves. Turn off the heat and let it stand for 5 minutes. Strain it through a fine mesh strainer and reserve for later.

method: cod

In a medium-sized frying pan, heat enough oil to just cover the base of the pan and set over high heat. Pat the skin of the cod dry with a paper towel, and season with an even sprinkling of salt and pepper. The patting-dry step will prevent the fish from sticking to the pan. Once the oil in the pan begins to smoke, place the fish gently in the pan with the skin side down. Let the fish cook for 30 seconds and lower the heat to medium. Cook them for 1 minute, and using a fish spatula or a thin metal spatula, lift the fish and move it slightly to ensure the skin is not sticking to the pan. Add the teaspoon of butter to the pan and cook for 2 more minutes. Turn the cod over onto the opposite side, and cook for 3 to 4 minutes. Check them every 30 seconds and cook until the fish is firm; if you want to peek inside, do it! The fish should be opaque and set firmly. Serve immediately.

plating

Either scoop out the bread pudding or cut a piece and place it on the plate next to the fish. If you have some watercress or wild arugula to garnish, it makes for a nice, fresh component and adds a lovely color. Drizzle the gastrique around the components, but be careful, as a little goes a long way with this sauce.

smoked haddock tartine

on toasted wheat bread, dill cream cheese, watercress, and cornichons

---

serves 4

4 fluid ounces melted butter

4 thick slices fresh wheat bread (if there is bakery nearby, buy their bread, as really good bread is worth it)

½ cup fresh dill, destemmed, chopped

Juice of 1 lemon

Zest of 1 lemon

8 ounces cream cheese, preferably organic

Salt and pepper, as desired

16 cornichons, halved lengthwise

1 pound of smoked Haddock (this is typically an East Coast thing, so smoked black cod or any smoked fish is a great substitution)

2 bunches watercress, destemmed

---

what to drink

- German Riesling
- Still rosé from Provence
- Pale ale
- Vodka and tonic with lemon

what to ask the fish guy

You probably don't need the fish guy for this one. Usually there is a refrigerated case close to the fish counter, and you should find what you are looking for there. If the fish guy has some smoked option not pre-packaged, ask where the fish is from and when it was smoked. Normally the fish will be brined or cured before smoking, which does extend the shelf life, but the fresher the better. If you go the prepackaged route, check the sell by date. Again, the fresher the better.

method

Preheat your oven to 425°F. Brush the melted butter on the bread, and lightly toast. In a mixing bowl, combine the dill, lemon juice, lemon zest, cream cheese, and a pinch of salt and pepper. Spread this mix evenly and generously on the toasted bread. Place the cornichon pieces, about eight per slice, evenly across the toasted bread. Break off little pieces of the smoked fish and scatter them evenly above the cornichons. Evenly place the watercress on top, and you're done!

plating

You have essentially done everything already. This simple recipe is a great one if you are in a hurry. Place the toasted bread on a plate and serve. As your dish is a tartine, another way to say "open-faced sandwich," there should be a fork and knife handy, just in case.

smoked salmon and farm egg frittata

with basil, lemon, chives, and tomato

serves 4

10 free-range or organic eggs (if farm-direct, the flavor's even better)

½ cup sour cream

Juice of 1 lemon

Zest of 1 lemon

2 teaspoons salt

1 teaspoon pepper

1 cup grated sharp cheddar cheese

½ pound Pacific or sockeye smoked salmon, sliced into thin strips

1 cup basil leaves, destemmed, torn

2 Tablespoons (½ bunch) fresh chives, diced

1 cup cherry tomatoes, halved lengthwise (reserve ½ cup for garnish)

2 Tablespoons cooking oil

1 Tablespoon unsalted butter

what to drink

- Blanc de blanc champagne
- Txakolina Rosé from Spain
- Your favorite daytime drinking beer
- Bloody Mary

what to ask the fish guy

You probably don't need the fish guy for this one. There is usually a refrigerated case close to the fish counter that will have what you are looking for. But, if the fish guy has some smoked fish options that are not pre-packaged, you can ask where the fish is from and when it was smoked. Normally, fish will be brined or cured before smoking. If you go the prepackaged route, check the sell by date; the fresher the better.

method

Preheat your oven to 400°F. In a mixing bowl, whisk together the eggs, sour cream, lemon juice, lemon zest, salt, pepper, and cheddar cheese. Using a wooden spoon or spatula, fold in the sliced smoked salmon, basil, chives, and ½ cup tomatoes. Heat a cast-iron skillet or nonstick pan over high heat and add the oil and butter. Once the butter has melted and the combination begins to slightly smoke, add the contents of the mixing bowl. Using a wooden spoon, stir everything in the pan in an effort to evenly distribute the garnish throughout the egg mixture. Cook for 3 minutes and place in the oven. Cook for 15 to 20 minutes or until the eggs are fully cooked. Remove from the oven and allow the frittata to cool for 2 to 3 minutes. Turn the frittata over onto a cutting board and serve.

plating

I usually cut this into pie-shaped slices. Add ½ cup of the sliced cherry tomatoes on the side to serve.

yellowfin tuna ceviche

with salted pear, basil, sesame, avocado, and salt and vinegar potato chips

serves 4

2 russet potatoes, washed well, thinly sliced

½ cup cooking oil

Salt and pepper, as desired

1 Tablespoon white wine vinegar

1½ pound handline caught yellowtail tuna, skin and bloodline removed, diced into ½-inch cubes

1 cup fresh lime juice

1 cup red onion, very thinly sliced

1 ripe pear, peeled, diced into very small pieces, seasoned with a pinch of salt

1 avocado, peeled, pit removed, diced into small pieces

½ cup of basil leaves, destemmed, chopped

½ cup of mint leaves, destemmed, chopped

1 Tablespoon sesame oil

1 Tablespoon soy sauce

2 Tablespoons olive oil

what to drink

- High quality cold sake
- Rosé champagne
- White ale
- Whiskey sour

what to ask the fish guy

Ask if they have #1 or #1+ grade tuna. #2+ is fine but usually has more waste. Make sure it is handline caught. Hawaiian longline and free school are reasonable second choices, but avoid the troll-caught stuff. Ask them to remove the skin and bloodline for you, as well. This will leave you with a ready-to-dice product. If they are not too busy and you seem to be getting along, you could even ask that they dice it for you into ½-inch cubes.

method

Preheat oven to 400°F. Toss sliced potatoes in with cooking oil and lay out as evenly as possible on a baking tray. Place in the oven. Turn them gently every few minutes and cook until evenly colored and crispy, approximately 8 to 10 minutes. Remove from the oven and place on a towel or paper bag to absorb the excess oil. Season with salt and pepper, as desired, and gently drizzle the vinegar as seasoning.

Place the diced tuna in a mixing bowl. Add the lime juice and red onion, and let it stand for 5 minutes. Add the pear, avocado, basil, mint, sesame oil, soy sauce, and olive oil. Taste it. Ceviche is very subjective, so if you think it needs more of something, go for it.

plating

This is an easy one. Put the chips in one bowl and the ceviche in another. It can be served individually or as something to share.

sautéed wild king salmon

with garlic cucumbers, roasted endive, and parsley butter sauce

serves 4

2 English cucumbers, peeled, seeds scraped out, thinly sliced

Salt and pepper, as desired

2 Tablespoons prepared roasted garlic

2 Tablespoons extra-virgin olive oil

2 Tablespoons champagne vinegar

2 endives, halved lengthwise

1 Tablespoon cooking oil

1 cup heavy whipping cream

Juice of 2 lemons

Zest of 2 lemons

2 cups unsalted butter, diced into small cubes, refrigerated

2 cups parsley leaves, destemmed

4 (5–6-ounce) wild king salmon portions

what to drink

- Un-oaked chardonnay
- Chablis
- French country ale
- Gin gimlet

what to ask the fish guy

Ask for 4 (5–6-ounce) portions of wild king salmon. Ask that the fish is scaled, skin left on, and pin bones removed. Later at home, if you feel one while gently moving your finger over the filet, you can easily wiggle it out.

method

Place cucumbers in a mixing bowl. Sprinkle salt and let them rest for 8 to 10 minutes or until you see liquid coming off of them. Squeeze to remove as much liquid as possible and dump what remains. Return the cucumbers to the bowl and mix in the garlic, olive oil, and champagne vinegar. Let this rest.

Preheat your oven to 375°F. Toss the endives in a bowl with cooking oil and a pinch of salt and pepper. Lay them flat on a baking sheet and place in the oven for 5 minutes. Remove the tray from the oven and turn the endives. Place in the oven for 5 more minutes and reserve for plating.

Place the heavy cream into a small sauce pot over medium heat. When it comes to a simmer, whisk it every 30 seconds and allow it to reduce by half its original volume. Add the lemon juice and zest and whisk for another 5 seconds. Slowly, add a few cubes of cold butter cubes and continue to whisk. When the butter has been whisked in, pour the butter sauce into a blender with the parsley leaves. Once the parsley is blended evenly, pour it back into the original sauce pot and keep at room temperature until plating.

Preheat a large sauté pan over medium heat. Season the salmon gently, lightly, and evenly with salt and pepper. Pat the skin dry with a paper towel. Add a small amount of cooking oil to the sauté pan, and when you see it slightly smoke, place the fish in the oil, skin-side down. Place the heat on high for 1 minute and then return it to medium. After 1 minute, gently lift the fish from the oil with a spatula, to ensure it is not sticking. Once it is able to move about the pan, lower the heat to medium-low, and watch as the salmon filets cook through the skin. When it appears that the filets are only slightly raw, turn them over and sear the other sides. You are ready to plate.

plating

Set a piece of endive on the plate. If the cucumbers have kicked off any more liquid, drain it off and place a scoop of the garlic cucumbers next to the endive. Place the salmon on top, and pour a generous amount of the parsley butter around the fish.

seared yellowfin tuna

with gingery carrots, tarragon parsnips, and tangerine vinaigrette

---

serves 4

Juice of 4 tangerines

Zest of 4 tangerines

1 teaspoon Dijon mustard

1 Tablespoon chili flakes

1 cup extra-virgin olive oil

Salt and pepper, as desired

1 pound baby carrots, peeled

Cooking oil, as desired

2 Tablespoons fresh ginger, peeled, grated

2 Tablespoons honey

2 dashes Tabasco

2 Tablespoons unsalted butter

1 pound parsnips, peeled, roughly chopped

4 (5-ounce) portions handline caught yellowfin ahi tuna

½ cup tarragon leaves, chopped

---

what to drink

- Albariño from Spain
- Gewürztraminer
- Pilsner
- Rum punch

what to ask the fish guy

Ask if they have #1 or #1+ grade tuna. #2+ is fine but usually has more waste. Make sure it is handline caught. Hawaiian longline and free school are reasonable second choices, but avoid the troll-caught stuff. Ask them to remove the skin and bloodline for you as well. This will leave you with a ready-to-dice product. Lastly, tell them about your plan, and ask if they can cut you blocks, not steaks, from the head side or the center of the loin.

method

In a mixing bowl, whisk the tangerine juice, zest, mustard, and chili flakes together. Slowly drizzle in the olive oil, whisking all the while. Adjust seasoning with salt and pepper, as desired, and reserve for later.

Preheat your oven to 350°F. Toss the baby carrots with some cooking oil and salt and place on a baking tray. Keep the dirty bowl handy. Roast the carrots until they are almost tender, 12 to 15 minutes. Then, return them to the mixing bowl and add the grated ginger, honey, Tabasco, and butter to the bowl. Place them back on the baking tray and back in the oven for 5 minutes. Reserve for later.

Place parsnips in cold water in a sauce pan and bring to a simmer. Cook for 3 minutes and strain. Place a frying pan over medium heat and add enough cooking oil to coat the bottom of the pan. Bring this to the point where it is about to smoke, and add in the parsnips. Lower the heat and gently finish cooking the parsnips by pan roasting. Cook for 3 to 4 minutes or until they are fork-tender. Turn off the heat, season with a pinch of salt and chopped tarragon leaves. Add the carrots to this pan and it's off to sear the tuna.

Season the tuna with salt and pepper. Place a medium frying pan over high heat, and add enough cooking oil to cover the bottom of the pan. When this is hot or beginning to smoke, place the tuna portions in the pan and stay with them with a pair of tongs in your hand. Move them after they have taken on a small amount of color, roughly 30 to 45 seconds on each side. Sear each side and remove from the pan.

plating

Place the carrots and parsnips in the center of each plate. Slice the tuna portions thinly with a sharp knife; a dull knife will damage them. Drizzle the vinaigrette around the plate and over the fish.

upside down pineapple cake

with lime curd, fresh pineapple, and basil

---

serves 4

upside down pineapple cake

½ cup melted butter

1 cup brown sugar, packed

1 ripe pineapple, peeled, core removed, sliced in ½-inch-thick wheel shapes (reserve some for garnish)

1 cup granulated sugar

1 cup unsalted butter, softened at room temperature

2 eggs

¾ cup heavy whipping cream

2 cups all-purpose flour

2 teaspoons baking powder

1 teaspoon ground cinnamon

1 teaspoon ground allspice

1 pinch salt

lime curd, fresh pineapple, and basil

1 cup granulated sugar

2 eggs

Lime curd

Juice of 5 limes

Zest of 5 limes

Remaining pineapple slices, diced, for garnish

½ cup basil leaves, destemmed, torn into small pieces

---

what to drink

- Demi-sec Champagne
- Moscato d'Asti
- Grand Marnier in a snifter

what to ask the fish guy

Not a whole lot to do here, but if you make the cake in advance, bring them a piece. They'll appreciate it!

method: upside down pineapple cake

Preheat your oven to 350°F. Mix the melted butter and brown sugar together and press into the bottom of a 9-inch cake pan or something similar in size. Add in the pineapple slices next to each other, 4 slices should fit depending on the size of the pineapple. Refrigerate for 1 hour. Mix 1 cup of granulated sugar and softened butter well. Whisk in two eggs one at a time, then whisk in the heavy cream.

In a separate bowl, mix the flour, baking powder, cinnamon, allspice, and salt. Gently fold the contents of the two bowls together. Pour this batter over the pineapple and brown sugar mixture in the pan. Bake for 25 to 30 minutes, checking every so often. When you are able stick a fork in it and the fork comes out clean, it's ready. Let cool for 15 minutes and turn it upside down.

method: lime curd

Whisk 1 cup of granulated sugar into the two eggs. Then, whisk in the lime juice and zest. Pour into a sauce pan and cook over a medium heat, whisking the whole time. When it thickens to a custard, it's ready.

plating

Cut a slice of cake and place on a plate. Add some diced fresh pineapple and sliced basil leaves. Complete each plate with a spoonful of lime curd and serve.

SPRING

baked oysters
with pernod, spinach, brie, and bacon / 53

clams on the half shell
with minted pea purée / 54

day-boat scallop ceviche
with grilled spring onions, lemon, crispy
cilantro, and rice paper crackers / 56

chilled mussel tea sandwiches
on brioche with curry aioli and
pancetta / 59

roasted haddock filet
with caramelized vidalia onions, frisée,
crispy artichokes, and bacon jam / 61

soft-shell crab blt
with lemon mayonnaise, first-of-the-season
tomatoes, iceberg lettuce, and bacon / 65

garlic prawns
with asparagus, orange, basil, and
escarole / 66

chilled lobster and udon noodle
with radish, radicchio, artichoke, lime,
sesame, and watercress / 69

grilled halibut
with mint, peas, fondant potatoes, and
spring onion soubise / 70

pan-fried petrale sole
with bagna cauda, mustard greens, and
grilled bread / 73

local sand dabs
with clementine, pistachio, asparagus, and
extra-virgin olive oil / 74

almond milk–poached rock cod
with oven fried potatoes, red currants, and
soft herb salad / 77

salt cod croquettes
with meyer lemon aioli / 79

skillet-roasted trout
with marinated radish, calamari, and spring
garlic vinaigrette / 81

chilled poached salmon
with field greens, asparagus, snow peas, and
green goddess dressing / 85

grilled tuna steak frites
with oven french fries, basil pistou, and red
wine and blueberry gastrique / 87

ginger and asparagus soup
with rock shrimp and mint / 91

yellowfin tuna crudo
with watercress, first-press olive oil, crispy
onions, sea salt, and lime / 92

poached albacore salad
with pea tendrils, fava leaves, and white
anchovy vinaigrette / 95

rhubarb and strawberry crisp
with cardamom whipped cream / 96

another fish tale

from a very southern place

"I'm sorry, I've never heard of Emeril Lagasse." This was my response to a recruiter as I strolled the career fair of my Alma Mater, The Culinary Institute of America, in 1999. I had my sights on either returning to New York City or moving to Sydney, Australia, as the Olympics were only a few months away and they were giving away visas as well as jobs. I would graduate at that exact time.

There was something compelling about this guy, though, and although his food was very specific and his new transition to television stole him away regularly, when I accepted the position in his kitchen, one could still feel his presence. Chef E, Chef, the Big Guy, etc. held command in and out of that building. The place was and is still massive. Hundreds of people arrived daily to devour his barbecue shrimp or andouille-crusted Texas Redfish. This style of cooking was new to me, but I loved it! We worked like maniacs, often beginning at nine o'clock in the morning until one o'clock the following morning. The team was a mix of locals and carpet baggers like me. It was a nightly battle, and this battle forged a team; many of us are still in touch today.

On Sunday, they allowed this army and this battleship of a restaurant to rest. Although competing with tourists for a bar stool wasn't my first choice, saddling up at The Crescent City Brew house on Decatur Street in the French Quarter was worth the effort. The raw or baked Plaquemine Parish oysters, seafood gumbo, and crawfish etouffé were perfect with their house brewed pilsner or wheat beer. But the thing I miss the most about New Orleans is the music; there was always music. I was happy to learn that Crescent City Brew house would live again post–Hurricane Katrina. I hope to sit with my wife and sons there one day, hopefully with an old friend from that battleship of a kitchen, and listen to live jazz while feasting on oysters and crawfish.

My Yankee ways were exposed when a friend invited me to my first crawfish boil. A large pot rolled with potatoes, spices, and corn. The baskets of crawfish were piled in and when it was ready, the lot was poured out onto our newspaper-covered picnic table. I was told to rip the head off, suck it, twist the tail, and bite out the meat. I didn't anticipate the uproarious laughter when this didn't go that well, but their southern hospitality kicked in soon after and we were twisting and sucking and laughing for hours. This gigantic mess of freshwater crustacean was the great equalizer. It was ninety-eight degrees at ten o'clock in the evening, but we laughed and feasted so long that the lingering smell of crawfish lasted through the next day. When in season, I buy these little mudbugs and serve them here in San Francisco. Mostly due to nostalgia.

The last bit about my time in the Deep South is a bit terrifying. I boarded what looked like a plank of wood for a fair price of twenty dollars. We disembarked from a small dock in Ascension Parish, Louisiana, just under an hour from New Orleans. Our questionable vessel set sail with a crew of one captain; I may be wrong, but his three-Budweiser breakfast influenced our mind-blowing conversation about shooting inanimate objects and would I be interested in having a turn? As this pre-dates the iPhone, I did not have a camera ready to capture his expression when I mentioned my lack of interest in guns. We found a commonality in our love of beer and seafood, so we pushed our way through the bayou, Captain Budweiser and me. I purchased a can of Bud from the captain for a buck, sat in my folding chair, and wondered why the hell we had a chicken in a cage on board. Once the passage of water broadened and we had passed a few small buildings of a village

still slightly underwater, we were in gator country. The antebellum plantations and cypress swamps quickly took a back seat to the feathered passenger who had joined the cruise as the main attraction. His cage opened and he foolishly ran to the perilous waters of the bayou. A threesome of gators could not resist, and as I choked on my Bud can, I was reminded that I was no longer in New York City. Only feathers were left, and I was very happy to be back on land and firing up my Volkswagen as I headed back to my flat in New Orleans only an hour later. Looking for a bite after a beyond interesting day, I made my way to Jaques-Imo's for the shrimp and alligator sausage cheesecake (selected to avenge the murder of my fallen fowl friend) and their blackened red fish with crab-chili hollandaise.

You simply have to love New Orleans for the rich history of music, food, fish, and being one of the most unique cities in this country. Springtime is best there, before the scorching summer arrives and, like in most temperate climates, this means fresh green vegetables, beautiful fish, love in the air, and healthier and lighter fare.

baked oysters*

with pernod, spinach, brie, and bacon

serves 4

6 strips Applewood smoked bacon, or
   your favorite kind

24 oysters

Salt, as desired

6 fluid ounces Pernod

½ pound baby spinach, washed,
   dried, thinly sliced

1 small wheel of Brie cheese, cut into
   24 little nuggets

what to drink

- Vintage champagne
- Pouilly-Fumé
- Flemish red ale
- Sazerac

what to ask the fish guy

Ask when the oysters were harvested. By law, they must keep shellfish tags on hand, so they should be able to assist. If the harvest date is more than five days ago, don't buy them. This doesn't mean they are necessarily bad, but the quality may be lesser. Unless you are visiting an oyster farm in Marshall, California, the likelihood of getting same-day oysters is slim. Up to four days is normally fine.

method

Preheat the oven to 375°F. Lay out the bacon on a baking tray lined with parchment or wax paper. Bake for 10 to 12 minutes or until cooked and slightly crispy. Let cool, break into 24 small pieces, and reserve for later. Under running cold water, scrub the oysters individually, focusing on the seam where the two shells meet. Many hardware stores and grocery stores carry "nail brushes." They double nicely as an oyster scrubber, but any medium to firm bristle-scrubbing brush will suffice. It doesn't need to be perfect, as a little sand won't hurt you. When the oysters are washed and scrubbed, it's time to shuck. It is best to refrigerate the cleaned oysters and allow for the mignonette to be ready. Use a kitchen towel to hold the oyster in place, and find the joint or small opening at the thickest end of the oyster where the two shells meet. Place the larger side of the oyster on a table, still using a towel to protect your hand and allow for a firm grip. Gently place the tip of an oyster knife into this joint. Wiggle it in until it clearly stops, and press down on the oyster to pop the top shell open (similar to opening a can of paint). Once it pops open, use the oyster knife to scrape it along the inside surface of the shell to cut the oyster away from the shell. Try not to lose any of the liquid—it is delicious!

On a baking tray, cover the bottom with salt. This will prevent the oysters from tipping over in the oven. Line them up on the salted tray and drizzle a teaspoon of Pernod into each one. Place a pinch of shaved spinach on top of each. Next, place a small piece of cooked bacon on each oyster. To finish assembling, place a nugget of Brie cheese on top. Place the oysters back in the oven for 5 minutes and serve immediately.

plating

Carefully transfer the oysters to a platter, as the shells can be quite hot. Have some small seafood forks ready, as it is best to use forks to eat the oysters. I recommend sipping the remaining liquid from the shell.

---

* This first Spring recipe is a twist on Oysters Rockefeller, which originated at the famous Antoine's in New Orleans, and was named after John D. Rockefeller, who was the richest man in the country at that time.

clams on the half shell

with minted pea purée

---

serves 6

1 cup frozen English peas, thawed to
    room temperature

Zest of 1 lemon

Juice of 1 lemon

¼ cup mint leaves, torn into pieces

¼ cup sparkling water or seltzer

1 Tablespoon extra-virgin olive oil

24 manila clams, or other small-
    format, hard shell clams

Salt, as desired

---

what to drink

- Prosecco from Valdobbiadene
- Grüner Veltliner
- Saison-style farmhouse ale
- Tom Collins

what to ask the fish guy

With all shellfish, my first question is "when was this harvested?" I usually give them a reasonable max of five days—if older than that, don't buy them. Make sure that you are not buying soft shell clams, quahogs, nor gaper clams for this recipe. They are better suited for different preparation.

method

We'll begin with the pea purée, as this dish is very simple and serves more as a passed hors d'oeuvres.

In a blender, add everything except for the clams and the salt (I know this is obvious, but there a lot of literal people out there). Adjust the seasoning with salt and perhaps more lemon, as desired, and reserve.

Wash the clams by scrubbing them well under running cold water. Let them rest in a bowl, submerged under running cold water; the idea here is to push out any and as much sand as possible. Strain the water, and let's get to shucking. Similar to shucking oysters, always use a towel to protect your hand so in the event the knife slips, you don't hurt yourself. If you have a clam knife, that's great, but you can get away with an oyster knife, as well. Hold the clam against the cutting board using the towel with the thickest end facing out. You will see a hinge-like point at the back of this shell. Gently cut the tip of the clam knife into this hinge, and pry it open a bit. Then, use the knife to scrape the clam from the shell, gently prying it open further as you go. Once fully open, scrape the clam from the shell at the point where it is connected. You will feel this as the knife passes between the muscle of the clam and the shell.

plating

Arrange the clams on a tray or individually as you see fit. Using a very small spoon, place a little dollop of the pea purée and serve immediately.

day-boat scallop ceviche

with grilled spring onions, lemon, crispy cilantro, and rice paper crackers

---

serves 4

4 sheets rice paper (also known as fresh spring roll wrappers)

10 day-boat scallops, roughly diced into ¼-inch pieces

Juice of 2 lemons

1 bunch spring onions or scallions

2 fluid ounces cooking oil

Salt and pepper, as desired

Zest of 2 lemons

½ bunch cilantro, destemmed, chopped

2 Tablespoons extra-virgin olive oil

1 Tablespoon red onion, peeled, minced

1 Tablespoon parsley leaves, destemmed, chopped

½ English cucumber, peeled, seeds removed, finely diced

½ bunch cilantro leaves, destemmed

---

what to drink

- Blanc de blanc champagne
- Pouilly-Fumé
- Kölsch
- Caipirinha

what to ask the fish guy

First, ask if they will clean them for you—in the US, scallops usually make it to market already cleaned, as many parts outside the obvious meat are not the most beautiful; many are quite delicious though, such as the roe. Next, ask if the scallops are previously frozen. It's not the end of the world if they are, but it makes cooking them a bit more challenging. You want fresh day-boat scallops. If they are from the northeast Atlantic seaboard, you found the best.

method

Turn the grill to high. If you don't have a grill, you can use a burner on the stove. Using a pair of tongs, hold the rice paper and pass it slowly back and forth over the heat. You will see it puff up. Keep passing it back and forth, without burning or turning it dark brown, until the whole thing has puffed; if any of it resembles its original form, it will be very unpleasant to eat. Set aside for later.

Place diced scallops in a bowl. Add the lemon juice and let it sit for 5 minutes. Toss the spring onions in cooking oil and a pinch of salt. Place on your grill or a hot pan and sear each side. Roughly chop into small pieces after they have been seared, and add this to the bowl. Now, add to the scallop and lemon juice mixture the lemon zest, chopped cilantro, extra-virgin olive oil, red onion, parsley, and cucumber. Adjust seasoning with salt and pepper. In a small sauce pan, heat ¼-inch deep amount of cooking oil. When it begins to smoke, add the cilantro leaves. Remove them after 30 to 45 seconds; you will know they are ready when the oil stops crackling. Please watch out that you don't get splattered with hot oil when the cilantro reacts with the oil. Turn the heat off, skim out the cilantro, and place on paper towels to absorb the oil. Sprinkle a little bit of salt and reserve for later.

plating

Break the rice paper into more manageable pieces and place in a bowl. Taste the ceviche one last time for seasoning, adjust if needed, and place into a separate bowl. Sprinkle the crispy cilantro pieces around and serve. I recommend spooning the ceviche onto each rice cracker and eating them like nachos.

chilled mussel tea sandwiches

on brioche with curry aioli and pancetta

---

serves 6

1 pound mussels

2 Tablespoons unsalted butter

2 whole shallots, peeled, thinly and evenly sliced

1 Tablespoon fresh thyme leaves, destemmed

6 fluid ounces white wine

1 clove garlic, thinly sliced

2 Tablespoons champagne vinegar

1 Tablespoon fresh lemon juice

1 egg

1 Tablespoon curry powder

Salt and pepper, as desired

4 fluid ounces olive oil

4 thin slices pancetta

1 (1-pound) loaf of brioche bread

½ cup dill fronds, destemmed, for garnish

---

what to drink

- Melon de Bourgogne
- Grüner Veltliner
- Belgian-style blonde ale
- Salty dog

what to ask the fish guy

Ask for PEI (Prince Edward Island) Mussels. To be honest, I lived with a few Canadians once upon a time, and I found them uncomfortably kind and annoyingly more organized, politically—but their mussels are the best. If you have willing fishmongers in front of you, ask if they are willing to debeard the mussels for you. The stringy little hairs that peek out of the mussel are inedible and referred to as the beard (technically, byssal threads, which allow them to attach to their surroundings). If the fishmongers won't debeard them for you, ask them to show you how. You need to wash each mussel, as they can be sandy, and then you need to grab those little fibers peeking out and gently wiggle them out.

method

Wash the mussels well under cold water, and gently tug the hairy looking stuff peeking out from the sides of the mussels; those hairs allow the mussels to hold on to rocks, and although harmless, they are unpleasant as a texture. In a sauce pot, add the unsalted butter and melt over medium heat. Next, add the shallots and cook over medium heat until the shallots are translucent. Add the thyme leaves, and the mussels right after. Cook for 30 seconds and then add the wine. Cover the pot and turn the heat to high. Cook for 3 to 4 minutes. They should start opening. With tongs in your hand, watch and individually pull them out of the liquid just as they open. Place them in a bowl. Once all of the mussels are out and open, let the liquid cool for 5 minutes while you scoop each mussel from the shell using a basic spoon. If some mussels do not open, discard them. Discard the shells, and strain the mussel broth over the mussels and refrigerate for at least 1 hour. Although not needed for this recipe, you can always freeze the mussel broth and use it again to make a soup or to steam shellfish at a later date.

In a blender or food processor, add the garlic, vinegar, and lemon juice. Mix for 1 minute and add the egg. Mix again for 1 minute. Add the curry powder and a pinch of salt and pepper. Continue to mix for 1 more minute. While this is mixing, as slowly as possible, drizzle in the olive oil. Once it has been added, taste and adjust with salt, pepper, and lemon juice as desired. Reserve for plating.

Preheat your oven to 350°F. Lay the slices of pancetta out on a baking tray lined with parchment or wax paper and place in the oven. Cook for 6 to 8 minutes. The pancetta will shrink in size greatly; the process is similar to cooking bacon, just faster.

Continued on page 60

Remove from the oven when the pancetta is crispy and dark in color while still not being burned. Keep the open on for plating.

plating

Slice the brioche into ½-inch thick slices and then into bite-sized rectangles. Lay these on a baking tray and toast in the oven for 3 minutes. Add a tiny spoonful of aioli to the top of each mini brioche toast. Set one of the chilled mussels in the aioli and top with a small piece of crispy pancetta. Place a small dill frond on top of each, assemble on a platter, and serve.

roasted haddock filet

with caramelized vidalia onions, frisée, crispy artichokes, and bacon jam

---

serves 4

4 slices of bacon, raw, small diced

1 whole shallot, peeled, minced

1 jalapeño pepper, stem and seeds removed, minced

½ cup sherry vinegar

½ cup honey

1 teaspoon fresh thyme leaves, destemmed

2 Vidalia onions, thinly sliced

6 fluid ounces cooking oil

2 artichokes*, thistle removed

4 fluid ounces olive oil

1 cup flour

Salt and pepper, as desired

4 (5-ounce) portions of haddock filet with the skin on, any sustainable cod will work as a substitution

1 teaspoon butter

1 head of frisée

---

what to drink

- Riesling
- Spätburgunder (German Pinot Noir)
- Sour beer, Gose
- Bourbon Manhattan

what to ask the fish guy

As with all cod family fish. ask for the thicker side of the haddock loin, and let them know you want the portions to be 5 ounces each. Although it might sound like you are asking a lot, ask them to leave the skin on and slightly score the skin down the middle. This shouldn't be a problem as they have the knives and they are cutting this for you anyway. By scoring the skin, the fish will cook more evenly as the skin will stay in the cooking oil throughout the process. If not, there is a good possibility that the fish will buckle or curve away from the oil, leaving the center uncooked.

method

In a small sauce pot, cook the bacon pieces until crispy. Add the shallot and jalapeño and cook for 30 seconds. Add the sherry vinegar and honey. Cook for 20 minutes over a low heat, then add the thyme leaves. Set aside for later.

In a frying pan, cook the sliced onions in 1 fluid ounce of cooking oil over medium heat. Season with a pinch of salt. When they start to simmer, lower the heat and cook for 30 to 40 minutes, stirring regularly to evenly caramelize the sugars in the onions. Once they are caramel in color and evenly cooked, remove from the pan and set aside for later.

Remove the exterior leaves of the artichokes and halve lengthwise. Cut away the rest of the leaves, and scoop out the thistles or fuzzy parts in the middle. Peel the stems, and place in olive oil in a small sauce pot. Over a medium to low heat, simmer until they are tender, approximately 20 minutes. Remove from the oil and cool . . . or just buy the jarred hearts. Slice and set aside to cool. Set a small pot of cooking oil, about ½-inch deep or 4 fluid ounces, on the stove over a medium heat, and bring to near the smoking point. Quickly toss the artichokes in flour lightly and place in the pot of hot oil. Fry for one minute and remove. Season lightly with salt and pepper and set aside.

In a medium-sized frying pan, heat 1 fluid ounce of cooking oil to just cover the base of the pan and set over high heat. Pat the skin of the haddock dry with a paper towel, and season with an even sprinkling of salt and pepper. The patting-dry step will prevent the fish from sticking to the pan. Once the oil in the pan begins to smoke, place the fish gently in the pan with the skin side down. Let the fish cook for 30 seconds and lower

61

---

*Good quality artichoke hearts in the jar make a fine substitution.

Continued on page 62

the heat to medium. Cook them for 1 minute, and using a fish spatula or a thin metal spatula, lift the fish and move it slightly to ensure the skin is not sticking to the pan. Add the teaspoon of butter to the pan and cook for 2 more minutes. Turn the cod over onto the opposite side, and cook for 3 to 4 minutes. Check them every 30 seconds and cook until the fish is firm; if you want to peek inside, do it! The fish should be opaque and set firmly. Serve immediately.

plating

Set some frisée on the plate and place some of the caramelized onions atop and around. Make small pools of warm bacon jam throughout. Place the cooked haddock on the frisée, then scatter the crispy artichokes around the plate.

soft-shell crab blt

with lemon mayonnaise, first-of-the-season tomatoes, iceberg lettuce, and bacon

serves 4

lemon mayonnaise

3 eggs

2 Tablespoons champagne vinegar

1 teaspoon salt

Juice of 1 lemon

Zest of 1 lemon

4 fluid ounces olive oil

Pepper, as desired

1 cup all-purpose flour

1 cup panko bread crumbs

2 fluid ounces cooking oil

4 soft-shell crabs, cleaned

8 thick slices sourdough bread

8 leaves iceberg lettuce, thinly sliced
  (similar to coleslaw)

2 whole ripe tomatoes

8 strips bacon, cooked, cooled

what to drink

- Pinot blanc
- Dry rosé
- Pale ale
- Pimm's Cup

what to ask the fish guy

The biggest thing is to ask them to clean them; this means cutting off their faces and the gills on both sides of the shells.

method

If you don't feel like making mayonnaise, that's okay. Go buy some and mix in lemon juice to your liking. But if we are making this from scratch, in a food processor or blender, combine 1 egg, vinegar, 1 teaspoon of salt, lemon juice, and lemon zest. Mix for 1 minute. Slowly drizzle in the olive while the machine is still mixing. Taste, adjust the seasoning with salt and pepper as desired, and reserve for later.

Set up a breading station with three bowls or shallow pans; one filled with flour, the second with 2 whisked eggs, and the third with bread crumbs. Drag the crabs through the flour, then pat them dry of any excess flour. Submerge them in the whisked egg mixture, transfer them over to the bread crumbs, and coat them evenly. Set a medium-sized frying pan with about a ¼-inch depth of cooking oil and heat over medium for 2 to 3 minutes; the oil should be around 350°F. Add the crabs to the oil and cook on one side for 3 minutes. Turn them over and continue cooking for another 3 minutes. Remove from the oil and turn off the heat. Season them lightly with a sprinkle of salt and pepper.

plating

Toast the sliced bread and lay out on a cutting board to build the sandwiches. Coat each slice evenly with the lemon mayonnaise. Lace the cooked crabs on the bottom row, and top each one with shredded lettuce, two slices of tomato, and two pieces of cooked bacon. Close the sandwich. I recommend sticking a skewer or long toothpick on the sides equidistant from one another and slicing down the middle. Set on plates and you're ready to serve.

garlic prawns

with asparagus, orange, basil, and escarole

serves 4

1 bunch asparagus, bottoms removed, chopped into ¾-inch pieces

1½ pounds 16/20 gulf prawns, peeled, deveined

3 cloves garlic, thinly sliced, sprout removed

½ cup olive oil

Salt and pepper, as desired

4 fluid ounces cooking oil

½ cup white wine

Juice of 1 lemon

Zest of 1 lemon

1 pound baby escarole, torn into 2-inch pieces

1 orange, cut into supremes or segments

1 Tablespoon parsley, destemmed, chopped

1 cup of basil, destemmed, torn into pieces

what to drink

- Vinho verde
- Pinot gris
- Crisp and light-style pilsner
- Mojito

what to ask the fish guy

Make sure you are buying wild gulf prawns from the Gulf of Mexico, preferably skim-net caught. Buy the peeled and deveined product. I love the 16/20 sizing. If you can find it, the U/9's are great (this means that less than 9 make up one pound). Avoid the farm-raised product from Asia. The methods are questionable and flavor is not nearly as delicious.

method

Set a large pot of lightly salted water to boil. Next to it, have a large bowl of ice water ready.

Boil the asparagus pieces for 3 to 4 minutes and move from the boiling water to the ice water. Once they are cooled, remove from the ice water and reserve until later. Mix the prawns, garlic, and the olive oil in a separate bowl, season with salt and pepper, and let stand for 15 minutes.

Set a large frying pan on high heat, drizzle a little cooking oil to cover the bottom of the pan, and add the prawns. Toss them around in the pan and when you see they've changed color and are beginning to curl, add the white wine. Simmer for 2 minutes, add the lemon juice and zest, and then set aside. Set another frying pan over high heat, and add cooking oil once again. This time, add enough to just cover the bottom of the pan and once it begins to smoke, add the blanched asparagus. Cook for 30 seconds and then add the escarole. Cook for another 30 seconds and remove from heat. Finish with the orange segments, chopped parsley, and salt and pepper as desired.

plating

Mix the escarole and asparagus combination well, add basil, and place on center of the plate. Place prawns on top of this mixture, and spoon the oil and liquid combination over the prawns and drizzle around the plate. Serve immediately.

chilled lobster and udon noodle

with radish, radicchio, artichoke, lime, sesame, and watercress

---

serves 4

1 (10-ounce) package dried udon
noodles

2 fluid ounces cooking oil

2 (1½-pound) Maine lobsters,
steamed, chilled, and meat
removed, or 1 pound cooked
lobster meat

2 artichokes, halved lengthwise,
exterior leaves removed, or 2 cups
jarred artichoke hearts, sliced

1 cup olive oil

1 bunch fresh radishes, washed,
quartered

1 head radicchio, halved, core
removed, shaved

2 cups watercress

3 Tablespoons sesame oil

2 Tablespoons soy sauce

Zest of 2 limes

Juice of 2 limes

Salt and pepper, as desired

---

what to drink

- Dry Riesling
- Hungarian tokay
- White ale
- Dark 'n stormy

what to ask the fish guy

Ask if the lobsters are from Maine
or at least the same New England
coast. They are the best. If they only
have spiny lobsters, that's okay too,
but don't expect any claws. If they
are willing to steam them for you, do
it; it's a lot less hassle and mess. Just
remember to tell them you will warm them up later, so a lighter
steaming is preferred.

method

Bring a large pot of water to a boil. Place the noodles in the pot
and cook, stirring regularly, for 10 to 12 minutes. Check them
every few minutes until they are soft and tender. When cooked
through, strain and rinse under cold running water. Toss with a
little cooking oil to prevent the noodles from sticking together,
and reserve for later.

If they won't cook the lobsters for you at the store, begin by
bringing a large pot of water to a boil. Set a large bowl of ice
water next to it. Have a large pair of tongs and a large spoon
ready. Now, have a look at the lobsters and make sure the rubber bands are still around their claws—it can be very interesting if they're not. Place them quickly into the unsalted boiling
water and use the tongs and spoon to dunk them. Keep a safe
distance, as they may flap their tail and splash some hot water
on you. Set your timer for 8 minutes. When the 8 minutes are
up, move the lobsters to the ice water. Let them cool for 10
minutes. Using a lobster cracker, crack the shells and dig out the
chilled meat. Chop into large pieces and set aside.

After removing the exterior leaves and cutting the artichoke
in half, cut away the rest of the leaves, and scoop out the fuzzy
part or thistle in the middle. Peel the stem and place in olive oil
in a small sauce pot. Over medium to low heat, simmer until
they are tender, approximately 20 minutes. Remove from the
oil and cool . . . or just buy the jarred hearts. Slice and set aside.
Combine the noodles, lobster, artichoke slices, radishes, radicchio, watercress, sesame oil, soy sauce, lime zest, and juice in a
mixing bowl. Mix well and taste. Adjust the seasoning with salt
and pepper and serve immediately.

plating

This dish works well when served family style, so a big bowl
with some serving utensils is the way to go.

grilled halibut

with mint, peas, fondant potatoes, and spring onion soubise

serves 4

½ pound unsalted butter + 2
    Tablespoons

1 bunch spring onions, roots
    removed, chopped

½ cup water

1 cup white wine

1 teaspoon ground clove

1 Tablespoon ground coriander

1 Tablespoon fresh parsley leaves,
    destemmed, chopped

Salt and pepper, as desired

1 pound marble or fingerling
    potatoes

2 thyme sprigs

1 bay leaf

2 fluid ounces cooking oil

4 (5-ounce) Alaskan halibut filets,
    skin off

1 cup frozen peas, thawed

½ cup fresh mint leaves, destemmed

what to drink

* Müller-Thurgau
* New Zealand sauvignon blanc
* Session IPA
* Cucumber gimlet

what to ask the fish guy

Ask for Alaskan Halibut. It is the most sustainable and yields the highest amount. Have her or him cut you 5-ounce portions and ask for the skin to be removed.

method

Soubise is a classic sauce based on a purée of onion. Begin by melting 2 tablespoons of butter in a pot and adding the chopped spring onions. Keep the temperature low, as we want the onions to slowly cook until they are tender. This should take 10 to 12 minutes. Then, add the water and wine and reduce until the volume of liquid is roughly half. Transfer this to a blender, and add the clove, coriander, fresh parsley, and a pinch of salt and pepper. Purée until smooth, but make sure your hand is covering the lid of the blender and protected by a towel. Set the soubise aside for later.

Place the potatoes in a shallow sauce pan and add the rest of the butter. Melt over a low heat. Once the potatoes are swimming in butter, add the thyme sprigs and the bay leaf. Simmer until the potatoes are tender, 15 to 20 minutes. Using a small knife, check for tenderness, and once tender, allow them to rest in the butter.

Turn on the grill, or get it ready (for all of you charcoal folks out there). Scrape it, brush it, and oil it well to prevent the fish from sticking to the grate. Generously rub all of the cooking oil over the fish and season gently with a sprinkling of salt and pepper. Place on the grill and let cook for 1 minute. Using a spatula, rotate a bit and continue cooking. Check to make sure it isn't too dark, as every grill is different. Keep cooking for 1 more minute and rotate again. Flip the fish over and repeat the process for 7 to 8 minutes or until the fish is cooked through. Remove from grill and set a large frying pan over high heat. Add the potatoes and a small amount of their butter to the pan, and cook for 3 minutes. Add the peas and remove from heat. Add the mint leaves and set aside. Gently heat up the soubise. Let's plate this!

plating

Place a mixture of potatoes, peas, and mint off-center of each plate. Place a portion of fish on top. In the empty half of the plate, make a pool of your warm soubise. Serve immediately.

pan-fried petrale sole

with bagna cauda, mustard greens, and grilled bread

---

serves 4

8 white anchovy filets, also known as Boquerónes

6 cloves garlic, crushed*

1 cup olive oil

Juice of 1 lemon

Salt and pepper, as desired

2 Tablespoons fresh parsley leaves, roughly chopped

1 loaf of fresh bread, sliced 1-inch thick

6 fluid ounces cooking oil

1 bunch mustard greens, destemmed, torn into large pieces

Zest of 1 lemon

1 Tablespoon marjoram leaves**

4 (5–6 ounce) petrale sole filets, skin off

---

what to drink

- Roero arneis
- Chardonnay
- Lager beer
- Vodka collins

what to ask the fish guy

Ask for petrale, but if they don't have it, sole or fluke are a good substitution. Ask to see if there is any skin attached or missed and to please remove it. If the filets are tiny, ask for a total of 1½ pounds of ready filets.

method

Combine anchovies, garlic, olive oil, lemon juice, and a pinch of salt and pepper in a food processor or blender. Blend for 15 to 20 seconds and transfer to a small pot. Place the pot on the stove and simmer on a low heat for 30 minutes. This is your bagna cauda, or "warm bath" in Italian. Finish with fresh parsley and set aside.

Grill or toast the bread and set it aside. Set a pan on the stove over a high heat, and add enough cooking oil to cover the bottom of the pan. Add the mustard greens, and using a wooden spoon, stir for 15 seconds. Remove from heat and add the lemon zest, marjoram leaves, and a pinch of salt and pepper. Set this aside while we cook the fish.

Place another frying pan or skillet over a medium to high heat. Add enough cooking oil to cover the bottom of the pan and heat until the pan begins to smoke. Pat the sole filets dry with a paper towel and season with a gentle sprinkling of salt and pepper. Place them in the pan and lower the heat to medium. Cook for 2 minutes and flip over. Cook for 2 more minutes and remove from the pan.

plating

Warm the bagna cauda, and place in a small bowl with a spoon. This is to share. On each plate, set a piece of grilled bread and top with the cooked mustard greens. Place the cooked filet of sole on top of that and serve. The idea is to cut a bite-size piece of bread, mustard, and fish, then either spoon the bagna cauda over it or dunk it. Your call!

---

*2 Tablespoons of prepared garlic is a good substitution.

**Oregano works as a substitution.

local sand dabs

with clementine, pistachio, asparagus, and extra-virgin olive oil

serves 4

1 bunch asparagus, cut into 2-inch pieces

3 clementines, peeled, segments pulled apart

1 cup salted and roasted pistachios, shelled

1 cup flour

4 fluid ounces very high quality extra-virgin olive oil

16 sand dabs, pan-ready

Salt and pepper, as desired

what to drink

- Albariño
- Viognier
- Hefeweizen
- Dirty martini

what to ask the fish guy

Ask that they have been cleaned and are pan-ready; they just have to make a small cut by the gills and scoop out the stuff that you do not want in your garbage can.

method

Bring a large pot of water to a boil and set a large bowl of water alongside of it. Cook the asparagus until tender, about 3 to 4 minutes, and set in the ice water. Once they have cooled, transfer to a mixing bowl.

Add the clementine segments and pistachios and set aside. Place the flour in a shallow pan or bowl and dredge the sand dabs in the flour. Pat them of any excess flour and set aside. In a large skillet or frying pan, add enough oil to create a ¼-inch depth and place over high heat. Once it begins to smoke, add the sand dabs and cook for 2 minutes. Turn them over and cook for 1 more minute. Remove from the pan. If the pan is small, keep it going as you may need to do this in 2 rounds. Finish cooking the fish, and get to plating.

plating

Mix the asparagus mixture and season as desired with salt and pepper. Place the cooked fish on top. Drizzle with a touch of very good extra-virgin olive oil and serve immediately.

almond milk–poached rock cod

with oven fried potatoes, red currants, and soft herb salad

serves 4

2 cups unsweetened almond milk

1 Tablespoon fresh ginger, grated

Juice of 1 lemon

Zest of 1 lemon

Salt and pepper, as desired

1 pound fingerling potatoes, cut into
   ¼-inch pieces

½ cup cooking oil

½ cup parsley leaves, destemmed

½ cup basil leaves, destemmed

½ bunch chives, cut into 1-inch
   match-sized pieces

2 teaspoons extra-virgin olive oil

4 (5-ounce) local rock cod filets,
   skinless

Red currants, as desired

what to drink

- Sauvignon blanc
- Amontillado sherry
- Brown ale
- Rum punch

what to ask the fish guy

Ask for the freshest local rock cod they have. Specify 4 portions roughly around 5 ounces or more after the skin is removed. If they don't have rock cod, Ling and Tru Cod are great substitutions. Avoid Pollock and Japanese Cod substitutions as they are inferior and the fishing practices are questionable.

method

Preheat your oven to 425°F. Place the almond milk, ginger, lemon juice and zest, and a pinch of salt in a medium-sized sauce pan and bring to a simmer. Toss the potatoes in the oil and lay out in a baking pan. Place the pan in the oven, and move the potatoes around every 3 to 4 minutes. Let them cook until golden brown and crispy, usually 15 to 20 minutes. Set aside for later. In a small mixing bowl, mix the herbs, extra-virgin olive oil, and a pinch of salt and pepper. Set this aside. Place the cod filets in the simmering almond milk and let them simmer for 5 to 6 minutes or until they are cooked all the way through. Taste the almond milk once the fish is cooked, and season with salt and pepper as desired.

plating

In soup bowls, place the fried potatoes in the center. Next, place the fish on top of the potatoes using a spatula. Pour as much of the almond milk broth as you wish in each bowl. Lastly, place a small amount of the herb salad and red currants on top of the fish and serve.

salt cod croquettes
with meyer lemon aioli

serves 6 (24 croquettes)

meyer lemon aioli

1 clove garlic, sprout removed, chopped

2 Tablespoons champagne vinegar

Juice of 1 Meyer lemon

Zest of 1 Meyer lemon

2 eggs

Salt and pepper, as desired

4 fluid ounces olive oil

salt cod croquettes

4 medium sized yukon gold potatoes, peeled and cut into quarters

Salt, as desired

¾ pound salt cod

½ cup heavy whipping cream

4 egg yolks

1 Tablespoon prepared roasted garlic

2 Tablespoons chives, diced

2 Tablespoons parsley, destemmed, chopped

Juice of 1 standard lemon

Zest of 1 standard lemon

1 teaspoon ground pepper

2 cups almond milk

2 cups all-purpose flour

4 eggs, beaten

2 cups bread crumbs

8 fluid ounces cooking oil

Zest of 1 Meyer lemon

Juice of 1 Meyer lemon

2 Tablespoons Dijon mustard

Watercress, for garnish

what to drink

- Blanc de blanc champagne
- Grüner Veltliner
- Saison-style ale
- Salty dog

what to ask the fish guy

You might be on your own here. Typically, you will find salt cod in a case next to the smoked fish products. If you cannot find it there, ask if they have it behind their counter, and where it's from. Avoid the Japanese and Russian products, as their fishing methods are questionable, and, as we know, the closer the source the better!

method: meyer lemon aioli

In a blender or food processor, add the garlic, vinegar, and Meyer lemon juice and zest. Mix for 1 minute and then add 2 eggs. Mix again for 1 minute. Add a pinch of salt and pepper. Continue to mix for 1 more minute. While this is mixing, as slowly as possible, drizzle in the olive oil. Once it has been added, taste and adjust with salt, pepper, and lemon juice as desired. Reserve for plating. If Meyer lemons are not available, regular lemons will do the trick.

method: salt cod croquettes

In a small pot, place the cut potatoes and cover with cold water. Add a pinch of salt and bring to a simmer. Cook this for approximately 20 minutes or until fork tender. Strain the water and allow to steam for 2 to 3 minutes. Then pass through a food mill, a potato ricer, or grab a wooden spoon and mash it up by hand the old fashioned way to make mashed potatoes. Reserve this at room temperature. Soak the salt cod in cold water for 4 to 5 hours. Change out the water after two hours. In a mixing bowl, whisk the cream, egg yolks, roasted garlic, chives, parsley, lemon juice, lemon zest, salt, and pepper together. Fold this mixture into the mashed potatoes and set it aside.

Continued on page 80

Set the almond milk in a pan on the stove and bring to simmer. Remove the cod from the water and pat it dry. Add it to the simmering milk. Cook for 10 to 12 minutes or until the cod is flaking and cooked through. Strain the milk, and place the cod in the bowl with the potato mixture. Gently fold the two together until mixed well. Chill for 1 hour. Set a 1-inch deep amount of oil in a pan and next to it, set a plate with paper towels; this is going to be your fryer. Take the cod and potato mixture from the fridge, and roll them into golf ball shaped spheres, roughly 1½ to 2 inches in diameter. Add them to the flour, patting off the excess flour gently, then place them in the 4 beaten eggs. Next, transfer them to the bread crumbs, and heat the oil until it almost is smoking. Fry the breaded balls for 2 minutes or until golden brown. It will probably take a few rounds to fry all of them. Set on the paper towels to absorb any excess oil.

plating

Lightly toss the watercress with a drizzle of olive oil and a squeeze of lemon. Place a spoonful of aioli on the center of the plate, and set the watercress on top. Place the croquettes however you like and serve. This can be done as a fork-and-knife experience and plated per person, but it also works well as a passed hors d'oeuvre.

skillet-roasted trout

with marinated radish, calamari, and spring garlic vinaigrette

serves 4

spring garlic vinaigrette

1 bunch spring garlic, roughly
    chopped

1 whole shallot, peeled, roughly
    chopped

½ cup champagne vinegar

1 cup extra-virgin olive oil

Juice of 1½ lemons

Zest of 1½ lemons

Salt and pepper, as desired

skillet-roasted trout

1 bunch French breakfast radishes,
    washed, tops removed, cut into
    ¼-inch pieces

Juice of 1½ lemon

Zest of 1½ lemon

½ pound fresh calamari tubes and
    tentacles, cleaned

4 fluid ounces cooking oil

2 Tablespoons extra-virgin olive oil

1 ripe tomato, cut into small wedges

1 Tablespoon fresh oregano,
    destemmed, chopped

1 bunch watercress, washed, stems
    removed

4 (5–6-ounce) trout filets, skin-on

what to drink

- A dry rosé from Provence
- Alvarinho from Portugal
- A light pilsner
- White sangria

what to ask the fish guy

If you are on the west coast, there are some great river trout options, such as mount lassen from the Sierra Nevada region. Occasionally, there are some good sea trout options, like steelhead and arctic char, but wild steelhead is protected in certain areas. The farm-raised versions are considered good options, too. Ask for 4 (5–6-ounce) portions, skin on, scaled, and pin bones removed. This will leave you with a ready-to-go portioned fish. When setting up the kitchen, check for those little pin bones again. They can gently be pulled out with needle-nose pliers if the fishmonger missed one.

method: spring garlic vinaigrette

In a food processor or blender, add the spring garlic, sliced shallot, champagne vinegar, 1 cup of olive oil, the lemon juice and zest, and a pinch of salt and pepper. Mix for 1 minute, agitate the contents, and mix again for another minute. Transfer this to small pot and reserve for later.

method: skillet-roasted trout

Soak the radishes in the lemon juice and zest for 1 hour. Roughly cut the calamari tubes into whatever shape pieces you like. Check the tentacles in the middle for a hard-feeling piece of cartilage as well as the eye. If present, simply pull them off. Set a frying pan over high heat, and add about 1 fluid ounce or just enough oil to cover the bottom of the pan. When the pan begins to smoke, add the calamari tentacles only. Cook them for 15 to 20 seconds and transfer them to the radish bowl. Reheat the same pan and repeat the process with the sliced tentacles only; this time, cook them for 5 seconds. Transfer them to the bowl with the radishes. Add the 2 tablespoons of extra-virgin olive oil, the tomato wedges, oregano, and watercress and reserve for later.

Preheat a large skillet over medium heat. If you don't have one, you can use a large frying pan

Season the trout gently, lightly, and evenly with salt and pepper. Pat the skin dry with a paper towel. Add a small amount of cooking oil to the skillet, and when you see it slightly smoke, place the fish in the oil skin side down. Increase the heat for

Continued on page 83

1 minute and return it to medium. After 1 minute, using a spatula, gently lift the fish from the oil to ensure that it is not sticking. Once it is able to move about the pan, lower the heat to medium-low and watch as the filet is cooked through the skin. When it appears that the filet is only slightly raw, turn it over and sear the other side for 10 seconds.

plating

Warm the sauce pot with the vinaigrette gently over a low to medium heat. Mix the calamari and radish salad and place on the plate. Place the fish on top of the salad. Drizzle the desired amount of vinaigrette around the plate and serve.

chilled poached salmon

with field greens, asparagus, snow peas, and green goddess dressing

---

serves 4

green goddess dressing

1 ripe avocado, pit removed, flesh
    scooped out

½ cup seltzer water

2 Tablespoons fresh tarragon,
    destemmed, roughly chopped

Juice of 1 lime

Zest of 1 lime

1 Tablespoon champagne vinegar

2 Tablespoons olive oil

2 teaspoons salt

1 teaspoon ground pepper

chilled poached salmon with field greens, asparagus, and snow peas

2 cups white wine

½ cup champagne vinegar

2 cups water

1 yellow onion, peeled, roughly
    chopped

2 thyme sprigs

2 parsley sprigs

1 bay leaf

1 pinch salt

4 (4–5-ounce) wild king salmon
    filets, skin off, already poached, if
    available

1 (5-ounce) bag spring lettuce mix

2 cups asparagus, cut into 1-inch
    pieces

2 cups snow peas, cleaned

what to drink

- Pinot grigio
- Chablis Premier Cru
- Kölsch
- The John Daly

what to ask the fish guy

Ask if they have any already-poached salmon. If they do, go for the thick pieces; they will have more moisture. If they don't, ask for 4 (4–5-ounce) portions of wild king salmon. Avoid all farm raised products, and remember that the Pacific wild king salmon is viewed as a more sustainable choice. Next, ask that the fish is scaled, skin left on, and that the pin bones are removed. You will want to check again when you are setting your kitchen that they pulled out all of the little pin bones. If you feel one while gently moving your finger over the filet, you can easily wiggle them out using a pair of needle-nose pliers.

method: green goddess dressing

In a blender, combine the avocado, seltzer water, tarragon, lime juice and zest, champagne vinegar, olive oil, salt and pepper and mix until smooth. Taste and adjust salt and pepper as desired. You may also prefer more lime or vinegar. Adjust that as well, if desired. Set aside for later.

method: chilled poached salmon with field greens, asparagus, and snow peas

Fish guys love poaching salmon. If they have some prepared, this dish will take no time at all to prepare. If not, combine the white wine, ½ cup champagne vinegar, water, chopped onion, thyme sprigs, parsley sprigs, bay leaf, and a pinch of salt in a deep sauce pan and bring to a simmer. Cook this for 30 minutes. Next, add the salmon to this liquid and gently simmer for 8 to 9 minutes, or until the salmon is a pink color and slightly firm to the touch. If you wish to check doneness, it's okay to peek inside and cook to your desired level of doneness. Remove from the liquid and set in the refrigerator.

Continued on page 86

Pick through the mixed greens for any wilted pieces. If your market has an open bin of mixed greens, you probably did this at the store already. Either way, check for quality and set in a mixing bowl. Set a large pot of salted water on the stove and next to it, set a large bowl of ice water. Once the water comes to a boil, add the cut asparagus and snow peas and cook for 2 to 3 minutes or until tender. You can also use green beans or snap peas as substitutions. Strain the veggies and submerge them in the ice water for 3 to 4 minutes, allowing them to cool. Strain them again, and add them to the bowl with the lettuce.

plating

Add a few spoonfuls of dressing to the lettuce bowl and mix. Taste for seasoning and adjust as desired. Place the salad on the plate. Place chilled salmon on top of salad. Another option is to flake the salmon and mix it in. Place a small dollop of dressing next to the salad and salmon as it is a lovely accompaniment and works very well as a dipping sauce for the salmon.

grilled tuna steak frites

with oven french fries, basil pistou, and red wine and blueberry gastrique

serves 4

red wine and blueberry gastrique

1 bottle inexpensive red wine

2 Tablespoons granulated sugar

1 whole shallot, peeled, sliced

½ cup blueberries, washed

½ cup red wine vinegar

1 Teaspoon cracked black pepper

1 pinch salt

1 Tablespoon fresh thyme leaves

grilled tuna steak frites with oven french fries and basil pistou

¾ cup olive oil

1 cup basil leaves

1 Tablespoon prepared roasted garlic

Zest of 1 lime

Juice of 1 lime

Salt and pepper, as desired

2 russet potatoes, or an 8-ounce bag of frozen French fries

4 (4–5-ounce) yellowfin ahi tuna steaks

what to drink

- Barbera d'Asti
- Russian River Pinot Noir
- Bière de Garde
- Rob Roy

what to ask the fish guy

Ask if they have #1 or #1+ grade tuna. #2+ is fine but usually has more waste. Next, make sure it is handline caught. Hawaiian longline and free school are reasonable second choices, but avoid the troll-caught stuff. Ask them to remove the skin and bloodline for you, as well. This will leave you with a ready-to-dice product. Lastly, tell them about your plan, and ask if they can cut thick steaks from the center of the loin.

method: red wine and blueberry gastrique

Open the wine and have a taste. You've already earned it! In a small saucepan, add the sugar and place over a medium heat. Stand there and watch as it slowly liquefies. It will soon begin to turn brown, and this is where you need to move quickly. Add the sliced shallots and blueberries to the light brown sugar and cook for 30 seconds. Then, add the vinegar and cracked black pepper. Simmer this until the pan is almost dry, approximately 4 to 5 minutes. Then, add the remaining red wine. Simmer this for 30 to 40 minutes or until it is a syrup-like in consistency. Regularly use a small spoon to test its thickness. Once it is ready, add a pinch of salt and the thyme leaves. Turn off the heat and let it stand for 5 minutes. Then, strain it through a fine mesh strainer and reserve for later.

method: grilled tuna steak frites with oven french fries and basil pistou

In a food processor or blender, combine the olive oil, basil, garlic, lime zest and juice, and a pinch of salt and pepper. Mix for 15 seconds and taste. Adjust seasoning and reserve for later. Preheat your oven to 425°F. Cut your potatoes into long wedges roughly ½-inch thick; if you're using frozen you're ready to go to the next step. Toss them in oil, and lay them out evenly on a baking tray. Cook for 8 to 10 minutes or until golden brown and turn them over so that they cook evenly. Cook for another 5 minutes or until they are equally brown and tender. Remove from the oven, drain off any excess oil, and season with salt and pepper as desired. Preheat your grill as hot as it will go. Scrape, brush, and oil it well; this will prevent the fish from sticking. Oil the tuna portions and lightly season them with salt and pepper. Place them on the grill and cook them for 1 minute. Turn them over and cook again for 1 minute. Remove from the grill. Let's plate this!

Continued on page 88

plating

Place fries on the center of the plate. Spoon small amounts of the pesto around the potatoes as you wish. Slice the tuna steaks and set next to the fries. Drizzle the gastrique very delicately and conservatively over everything; you can always add more if you choose. You are ready to serve.

ginger and asparagus soup

with rock shrimp and mint

serves 4

- 2 fluid ounces cooking oil
- 1 leek, white part only, roughly chopped
- 2 whole shallots, peeled, roughly chopped
- 2 Tablespoons fresh ginger, grated
- 1 medium-sized yellow onion, peeled, sliced
- 1 Tablespoon unsalted butter
- 2 bunches asparagus, stems removed, roughly chopped
- 2 cups white wine
- 3 cups water
- ½ cup heavy whipping cream
- 2 Tablespoons white rice
- 1 cup (8 leaves) fresh mint, destemmed
- Juice of 1 lemon
- Zest of 1 lemon
- Juice of 1 lime
- Zest of 1 lime
- Salt and pepper, as desired
- ½ pound fresh rock shrimp

what to drink

- Brut Champagne
- Gruener Vetliner
- German pilsner
- Botanical gin fizz

what to ask the fish guy

This is very straightforward, as nobody sells these with the shells on. Fresh wins every time, so ask when they were caught, and the more recent the better. Anything over 5 to 6 days and you might want to consider a different garnish for the soup.

method

In a large pot, cover the bottom with 1 fluid ounce of cooking oil and heat on high. As it is just about to smoke, add the leek, shallots, and onion and turn the heat down to low-medium. Add the butter and stir regularly until the contents of the pot are soft and translucent. The idea is to cook them through while taking on as little color as possible, approximately 12 to 15 minutes. Turn the heat to medium and add the asparagus. Keep stirring. Cook the asparagus for 3-4 minutes and add the white wine. Let that simmer for 3 more minutes, and add the water and heavy cream. Bring that to a boil and add the white rice. Cook for 12 minutes, ensuring the rice is soft, and then add the mint, lemon juice and zest, and lime juice and zest. Remove from the stove and in batches, purée in the blender until it is smooth. Once it is all puréed, adjust seasoning with salt and pepper and refrigerate for 2 hours or until chilled. Taste it again and adjust seasoning if desired. This will be served cold.

Now, set a frying pan over high heat and coat the bottom with 1 fluid ounce of cooking oil. When it begins to smoke, add the rock shrimp and stir them around in the pan. Cook for 1½ to 2 minutes and reserve for plating.

plating

Place the shrimp equally amongst the bowls. Pour the chilled soup in with the shrimp. Finish with fresh mint leaves and serve.

yellowfin tuna crudo

with watercress, first-press olive oil, crispy onions, sea salt, and lime

serves 4

4 fluid ounces cooking oil

1 cup flour

1 teaspoon cayenne pepper

1 medium onion, peeled, thinly sliced

¾ pound yellowfin ahi tuna

2 Tablespoons first-press olive oil*

1 teaspoon flaky sea salt (Maldon is a
   great option)

Juice of 1 lime

1 bunch watercress

Sea salt, as desired

what to drink

- Rosé champagne
- Daiginjo sake
- Lager from Asia
- Old Cuban

what to ask the fish guy

Ask if they have #1 or #1+ grade tuna. #2+ is fine but usually has more waste. Make sure it is handline caught. Hawaiian longline and free school are reasonable second choices, but avoid the troll-caught stuff. Ask them to remove the skin and bloodline for you, as well. This will leave you with a ready-to-dice product. If they are not too busy and you seem to be getting along, you could even ask that they thinly slice it for you sashimi style; you can always claim that you were just kidding when they look at you as if you are crazy.

method

Set a pot with all of the cooking oil on the stove over medium heat—this will serve as your fryer. If you have a deep fryer, that is a great decision you made, so use that instead. Mix the flour and the cayenne pepper in a mixing bowl. Heat the oil until it just begins smoking, add the onions, and turn the heat to low-medium. Cook the onions for 2 to 3 minutes or until golden brown and crispy. Set on paper towels to absorb the excess oil, and reserve for plating. Next, and with a sharp knife, slice the tuna as thinly as possible. Set it aside for plating.

plating

Arrange the tuna slices on the plate as you choose. Drizzle the first-press oil over the fish gently and conservatively, less than a teaspoon each. Drizzle the lime juice in the same fashion as above. Arrange the undressed watercress as you choose. Place a small pinch of sea salt on each fish, and then top with the crispy onions. You are all set.

---

*Olio verde and cold-press extra-virgin olive oil are good substitutions.

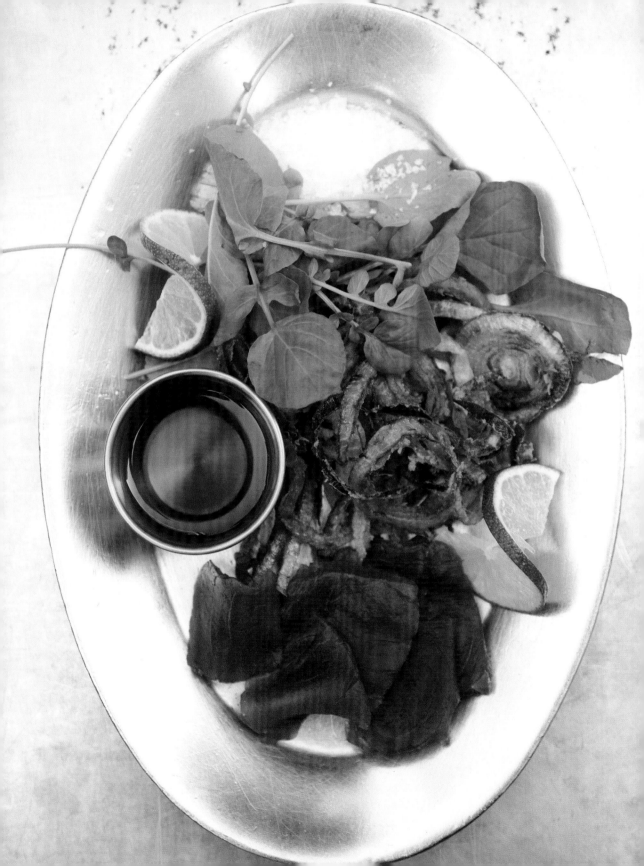

poached albacore salad

with pea tendrils, fava leaves, and white anchovy vinaigrette

serves 4

poached albacore salad with pea tendrils and fava leaves

1 cup olive oil

2 cloves garlic, crushed

1 bay leaf

1 Tablespoon parsley stems

4 (4–5-ounce) portions of albacore loin

2 handfuls pea tendrils

2 cups fava leaves, destemmed

white anchovy vinaigrette

1 cup extra-virgin olive oil

½ cup red wine vinegar

8 white anchovies

1 Tablespoon prepared roasted garlic

1 Tablespoon parsley leaves, destemmed, roughly chopped

Zest of 1 lemon

Juice of 1 lemon

1 Tablespoon Dijon mustard

Salt and pepper, as desired

what to drink

- Spanish Verdejo
- California sauvignon blanc
- Session IPA
- Sherry cocktail

what to ask the fish guy

Oddly enough, albacore is one of the few fishes that can handle being frozen. If it was previously frozen, ask if it was blast frozen at sea. This is the best way. If it's fresh, that's great too. Also, Oregon and California are fishing some great albacore, so always go the domestic route. It's tough to argue that fresh and local are always the best choice.

method: poached albacore salad with pea tendrils and fava leaves

In a medium pan, combine the olive oil, garlic, bay leaf, and parsley stems, and simmer for 10 minutes on a low heat. Place the albacore portions in the hot oil and cook for 6 minutes or until medium. Make sure the fish is submerged. Remove the albacore and refrigerate. Wash the pea tendrils and fava leaves in cold running water. Let them dry on a towel for 3 to 4 minutes, then pat them dry. Remove the albacore from the refrigerator, and slice each portion into ½-inch slices.

method: white anchovy vinaigrette

In a blender, combine the extra-virgin olive oil, red wine vinegar, white anchovies, roasted garlic, parsley leaves, lemon zest and juice, and mustard. Blend for 2 minutes or until smooth. Adjust seasoning with salt, pepper, and lemon as desired. Set aside for plating.

plating

In a mixing bowl, mix the leaves with enough dressing to just barely coat them. Set this on the middle of the plate, and arrange the sliced albacore on top. Drizzle a little of the vinaigrette around the plate and over the fish. Serve.

rhubarb and strawberry crisp

with cardamom whipped cream

---

serves 4

1 cup + ¼ cup granulated sugar

½ cup brown sugar

2 cups all-purpose flour

½ pound + ¼ pound unsalted butter, cubed, refrigerated

4 cups strawberries, tops cut off, cut into ¼-inch pieces

2 cups rhubarb, cut into 1-inch pieces

1 teaspoon ground cinnamon

Zest of 1 orange

Juice of 1 orange

½ cup heavy whipping cream

1 Tablespoon ground cardamom

what to drink with this dish

- Bracchetto d'Acqui
- Demi-Sec Champagne
- A berry-based Lambic
- Strawberry Bellini

what to ask the fish guy

Where is the rhubarb?

method:

In a food processor or by hand in a mixing bowl, combine ¼ cup of granulated sugar, brown sugar, and all-purpose flour. Add ½ pound of cubed butter to the mix. Ultimately, as it begins to mix, it will transform into pearl sized balls. Stop at that point to avoid making a solid mass. Refrigerate for 10 to 15 minutes

In a separate mixing bowl, mix the strawberries, rhubarb, 1 cup of granulated sugar, cinnamon, and the orange zest and juice and set this aside for a moment. Use the remaining butter to grease your baking dish or individual dishes. Preheat the oven to 350°F.

Spoon the mix to just shy of about ¼-inch from the top of the cooking dish; a 9 x 9-inch pan or individual ramekins both work very well. Pack a ¼-inch thick layer of streusel on top of this and place in the oven. Bake for 20 to 25 minutes or until the streusel is dark brown and crispy. You should see the liquid from the fruit bubbling a bit. Let it cool for 5 to 10 minutes and serve warm.

In an electric mixer with the whisk attachment or in a mixing bowl with a whisk, slowly whip the cream until it begins to thicken. Increase your speed at this point until it is light and fluffy. Whisk in the cardamom and set aside.

plating

Either scoop out the desired portion size or serve the individuals. Spoon as much whipped cream as you would like on top, and that's it. You're ready.

SUMMER

oyster ceviche
with summer melon, cucumber, red onion,
and chervil / 103

shandy-steamed steamer clams
with ginger butter and fresh bread / 104

grilled scallops
with mashed avocado, arugula, roasted
shallots, and hazelnut oil / 107

steamed mussel chowder
with baguette croutons / 108

poached lobster
with local corn, asparagus, salt-roasted little
potatoes, herbs, and drawn butter / 111

grilled prawn salad
with mango, Napa cabbage, mint, basil,
cucumber, and coconut vinaigrette / 112

dungeness crab rolls
on hot dog buns with lemon and fried
pickles / 115

shrimp and coconut soup
with basil, ginger, and roasted cremini
mushroom / 116

grilled halibut
with sweet corn stew, pea tendrils, and
tomato vinaigrette / 119

pan-fried petrale sole
with raw heirloom tomato sauce, torn basil,
and caper berries / 120

baked local sole
with a shaved zucchini and olive salad and
roasted red pepper coulis / 123

pan-seared tru cod
with salted cantaloupe, sweet corn, cherry
tomato, verbena, and oregano / 124

the cod melt
with sharp cheddar, dijon, grilled local cod,
and brioche / 127

grilled wild king salmon
with cherry tomato, sweet corn, crushed
cucumbers, and oregano / 128

smoked trout salad
with summer herbs and mojito vinaigrette / 131

salmon burgers
with heirloom tomato, sweet gem lettuce,
and creole mustard / 132

the timeless tuna tartare
with pineapple, cucumber, soy sauce,
cilantro, and sesame crackers / 135

sweet corn and blueberry pound cake
with strawberry salsa and strawberry basil
sauce / 136

a fish tale about hawaii

that place inspires summer recipes

I've been there twice, so please understand that I am far from an expert on Hawaiian cuisine, culture, or pretty much anything else Hawaiian. But, simply put, Hawaii is the most beautiful of places! Some may prefer the mountains and canyons that span this great country, or the forests, bayous, deltas, and their nearby coastlines, but I will ask each of them if they have ever experienced the Hawaiian Islands, because there is magic there. Yes, I've only been twice, but getting me back on that plane each time was always worth the effort. Prior to my family's arrival, I learned of how prolific the fast food culture is, how processed meats in a can are a staple, and of the rising health concerns per capita due to the poor diet of the locals. After swallowing the mystifying beauty that surrounded us and sipping a mai tai inspired by my then two-year-old's travel demeanor, we settled in. Throughout our travels, we avoided the resorts and the mainstream stuff. It was that real island sense of aloha that created the magic for us. In searching for the real island experience, a few chats with some locals led us to a fish store that offered the local catch each morning. When we found that first fish store, the

folks selling their catch were happy to scale and clean whatever we wanted. Even though I knew how to do it myself, I asked them to gut and filet these amazing selections from the sea, as I was without my knives and a smart place to butcher this amazing seafood (not sure my family would have loved that in our tiny rental bathroom!). This saved time and made for some fantastic outdoor grilling. The search was almost as fun as the meal, and we learned the true meaning of aloha, apart from hello (not giving it away, so you'll have to find out for yourself!). Anyway, there was nothing better than serving the fresh-caught tuna, monchong, ono, or opakapaka from a grill on the beach to our picnic table while seeing the humpback whales crest, lobtail, and breech, and I am not exaggerating. Some local pineapple to make a salsa, the fragrant local lager for the adults, a fresh green salad included, and this made for a series of memorable dinners for four. The allure of the tropics was the distant dance, journey, and the humpback whales surely didn't hurt. Make sure you visit during humpback season, avoid SPAM (the canned meat), hang with some locals, and make your own food. It's worth it!

oyster ceviche

with summer melon, cucumber, red onion, and chervil

---

serves 4

24 of the best oysters you can find (I love Kumamoto oysters)

Zest of 4 limes

Juice of 4 limes

1 cup English cucumber, peeled, seeds removed, ribboned

2 Tablespoons extra-virgin olive oil

1 cup red onion, peeled, thinly shaved

2 cups ripe summer melon, peeled, seeds removed, cut into small chunks

1 Tablespoon cracked black pepper

1 Tablespoon fresh mint leaves, destemmed, thinly sliced

½ bunch chervil leaves, destemmed

---

what to drink

- Brut champagne
- Melon de Bourgogne (Muscadet)
- Pilsner
- Margarita on the rocks, no salt

what to ask the fish guy

Ask when the oysters were harvested. By law, they must keep shellfish tags on hand, so they should be able to assist. If the harvest date is more than five days ago, don't buy them. This doesn't mean they are necessarily bad, but the quality may be lesser. Unless you are visiting an oyster farm in Marshall, California, the likelihood of getting same-day oysters is slim. Up to four days is normally fine.

method

Wash and shuck the oysters first. Here's a reminder as to how: we start by washing them. Many hardware stores and grocery stores carry "nail brushes." They double nicely as an oyster scrubber, but any medium to firm bristle-scrubbing brush will suffice. Under running cold water, scrub the oysters individually, focusing on the seam where the two shells meet. It doesn't need to be perfect, as a little sand won't hurt you. When the oysters are washed and scrubbed, it's time to shuck. Use a kitchen towel to hold the oyster in place, and find the joint or small opening at the thickest end of the oyster where the two shells meet. Place the larger side of the oyster on a table, still using a towel to protect your hand and allow for a firm grip. Gently place the tip of an oyster knife into this joint. Wiggle it in until it clearly stops, and press down on the oyster to pop the top shell open (similar to opening a can of paint). Once it pops open, use the oyster knife to scrape it along the inside surface of the shell to cut the oyster away from the shell. Try not to lose any of the liquid—it is delicious! Place the zest and juice of lime in a mixing bowl, and add the shucked oysters and their liquid to the lime juice. Discard the shells. Add the thinly shaved red onion, and let this rest for 15 minutes. Add the extra-virgin olive oil, and you're ready to plate.

plating

Place the ribbons of cucumber on the plate. Set the melon pieces on the cucumber, then place the oysters on the plate as you wish. Hang on to the liquid. Sprinkle the cracked pepper and mint on everything, and place the chervil leaves on top. Drizzle a small amount of the ceviche liquid and serve.

shandy-steamed steamer clams

with ginger butter and fresh bread

serves 4

ginger butter

1 pound unsalted butter

4 Tablespoons grated ginger

Juice of 1 lemon

Zest of 1 lemon

1 pinch salt

clams

2 pounds soft-shell steamer clams*

2 (12-ounce) bottles pilsner beer

12 ounces lemonade

1 pinch pepper

2 Tablespoons unsalted butter

1 loaf fresh bread, nothing too dark or sour

what to drink

- Champagne, any kind
- Pinot blanc
- A shandy
- Greyhound

what to ask the fish guy

With all shellfish, my first question is "when was this harvested?" I usually give them a reasonable max of five days—if older than that, don't buy them. Soft-shell steamer clams are native to New England, but they make their way around because of demand. If they smell off, don't buy them. If they have opened a little bit, ask the guy to tap one on the table and see if it closes; if it does, it means they are still alive and you will be fine.

method: ginger butter

Melt butter with ginger, and simmer for 5 minutes over a low heat. Add the lemon juice, lemon zest, and a pinch of salt. Keep at room temperature and reserve for later.

method: clams

Place clams in a bowl and sit beneath cold running water; let them sit there for 10 minutes, then move them around to try and get rid of any sand that may still be present. The downside, and only downside, is that it's impossible to remove all of the sand; you will be eating some sand, but it is absolutely worth it. In a tall pot, combine the beer, lemonade, and a pinch of pepper. Bring this to a raging boil and add the clams. Cover the pot quickly and cook for 5 minutes. Watch as the clams begin to open. Remove them individually once they have opened and place in a serving bowl.

plating

Make sure you have plenty of napkins; this is going to get messy. Place the serving bowl in the middle of the table, and place a separate bowl next to it for discarding the shells. Place the broth in individual bowls for everyone, and place the butter in individual bowls for everyone, as well. The big idea here is that you are washing the clam in the broth of any excess sand, dunking it in the butter, and then sucking it down like an animal. It's a blast. Set the fresh bread out so people can dunk it in the broth or butter.

grilled scallops

with mashed avocado, arugula, roasted shallots, and hazelnut oil

---

serves 4

6 whole shallots, peeled, halved

2 fluid ounces cooking oil

Juice of 2 limes

Zest of 2 limes

1 Tablespoon fresh cilantro leaves, destemmed, roughly chopped

2 ripe avocados, pits removed

Salt and pepper, as desired

12 day-boat scallops, U-10 are the perfect size

¼ pound wild arugula

2 Tablespoons of hazelnut oil

---

what to drink

- Vintage champagne
- White burgundy
- Hefeweizen
- Margarita on the rocks, no salt

what to ask the fish guy

First, ask if they will clean them for you—in the US, scallops usually make it to market already cleaned, as many parts outside the obvious meat are not the most beautiful; many are quite delicious though, such as the roe. Next, ask if the scallops are previously frozen. It's not the end of world if they are, but it makes cooking them a bit more challenging. You want fresh day-boat scallops. If they are from the northeast Atlantic seaboard, you found the best.

method

Preheat the oven to 350°F. Toss the halved shallots in 1 fluid ounce of cooking oil and place on a baking tray. Place in oven, and move them around every 5 minutes. Cook for 20 minutes or until lightly brown and tender. Reserve for later. In a mixing bowl, add the lime juice, lime zest, and cilantro. Scoop out the avocado and place in the same bowl. With a wooden spoon, mash it up. Taste and adjust seasoning with salt and pepper as desired; approximately ½ teaspoon of each should do it. Set this aside for later.

Turn on the grill and get it hot. Scrape it clean, brush it even cleaner, and oil it generously. Lightly rub the remaining cooking oil on the scallops and season lightly with salt and pepper. Place them on the hot grill and move them every few seconds. Cook on the same side for 1½ minutes and flip them over. While still moving them around the grill, cook for another 1½ minutes and remove from the grill. They will still feel a bit raw, which is what you want. If you want to cook them more, you can, but don't blame me for the dry and stringy end result.

plating

In the center of the plate, set a scoop of mashed avocado. Set a few pieces of roasted shallots on top.

Next, place a small handful of raw arugula on top. Place the scallops on the arugula, drizzle the hazelnut oil around the plate, and serve immediately.

steamed mussel chowder

with baguette croutons

---

serves 4

2 fluid ounces cooking oil

1 leek, white part only, diced small

1 medium-sized yellow onion, diced small

2 whole shallots, peeled, diced small

2 pounds mussels, washed, debearded

1 (750 ml) bottle white wine

1 medium-sized Yukon gold potato, peeled, diced into ½-inch pieces

½ cup cooked corn, frozen or cut off the cob

2 cups heavy whipping cream

1 Tablespoon cornstarch

2 Tablespoons water

1 Tablespoon chives, small diced

1 Tablespoon fresh dill, destemmed, roughly chopped

Juice of 2 lemons

Zest of 2 lemons

Salt and pepper, as desired

½ baguette, cubed

3 Tablespoons extra-virgin olive oil

---

what to drink

- Chardonnay
- Soave classico
- Belgian triple
- Vodka lemonade

what to ask the fish guy

Ask for PEI (Prince Edward Island) Mussels. To be honest, I lived with a few Canadians once upon a time, and I found them uncomfortably kind and annoyingly more organized, politically— but their mussels are the best. If you have willing fishmongers in front of you, ask if they are willing to debeard the mussels for you. The stringy little hairs that peek out of the mussel are inedible and referred to as the beard (technically, byssal threads, which allow them to attach to their surroundings). If the fishmongers won't debeard them for you, ask them then to show you how. You need to wash each mussel, as they can be sandy, and then you need to grab those little fibers peeking out and gently wiggle them out.

method

In a tall pot, add the cooking oil and place over medium-high heat. When the oil is about to smoke, add the leek, onion, and shallots. Lower the temperature to medium and move everything around with a wooden spoon. Cook for 3 to 4 minutes and add the cleaned mussels (see what to ask the fish guy). Stir the mussels in the pot and add the wine; have a sip to make sure it's okay first. Cover the pot and let it come to a boil. After 3 to 4 minutes, the mussels should start opening. Stand there and remove them as they open; a few may not, which is normal. Discard those that do not open. Once all mussels are out and open, scoop them out of their shells and place in a bowl. If there are any pieces of leek or onion out of the pot, return them to the pot along with any liquid the mussels may have brought with them. Let the broth cook for 10 minutes, gently simmering but not boiling. Add the potatoes to the broth and cook for 8 to 10 minutes or until they begin to soften; check softness by poking them with a small knife. Add the corn and the cream and cook for 10 more minutes. Combine the cornstarch and water and stir into the pot; this will help thicken the chowder. Add the chives, dill, lemon juice, and lemon zest. Adjust seasoning as desired with salt and pepper. You're done.

Preheat the oven to 375°F. Toss the baguette croutons with the olive oil, a pinch of salt and pepper, and arrange evenly on a baking tray. Bake for 5 to 6 minutes or until they just start to turn brown. They should still be still; fresh bread croutons are the best and aren't awkward like store-bought dry croutons.

plating

Using a big ladle or spoon, stir the chowder and place in bowls, making sure each has an equal amount of broth and veggies. Place a few mussels in each bowl and sprinkle some croutons on top to serve.

poached lobster

with local corn, asparagus, salt-roasted little potatoes, herbs, and drawn butter

---

serves 4

4 (1½-pound) live or already steamed Maine lobsters

1 pound mixed marble or fingerling potatoes

2 fluid ounces cooking oil

Salt and pepper, as desired

4 ears of corn on the cob, shucked

1 pound + 4 Tablespoons of unsalted butter

1 pound asparagus, cut into 1 inch sections

1 cup parsley leaves, destemmed

½ cup cilantro leaves, destemmed

½ cup basil leaves, destemmed, torn into pieces

---

what to drink

* Blanc de blanc champagne
* Bandol rosé
* Golden ale
* Pisco punch

what to ask the fish guy

Ask if the lobsters are from Maine or at least the same New England coast. They are the best. If they only have spiny lobsters, that's okay too, but don't expect any claws. If they are willing to steam them for you, do it; it's a lot less hassle and mess. Just remember to tell them you will warm them up later, so a lighter steaming is preferred.

method

Place a large pot of water over high heat and boil. Set a large bowl of ice and water close by. Have a large pair of tongs and a large spoon ready. Now, let's cook the lobsters. Look at the lobsters and make sure the rubber bands are still around their claws—it can be very interesting if not! Place them quickly into the unsalted boiling water and use the tongs and spoon to dunk them. Keep a safe distance as they may flap their tail and splash some hot water on you. Set your timer for 8 minutes. When the 8 minutes are up, move the lobsters to the ice water. Reserve lobster water for plating.

Preheat your oven to 350°F. Using a baking tray, cover the bottom with a lot of salt. Set the potatoes nestled in the salt, and cover them with more salt. Bake for 30 to 40 minutes or until they are soft. Begin checking them around 20 minutes as all ovens are different and water content in potatoes can vary. Remove from the heat and let them cool a bit. Brush the salt off and reserve for later.

Keep the oven on. Rub the cleaned corn on the cob with the 4 tablespoons of unsalted butter, and season lightly with salt and pepper. Toss the asparagus in a bit of oil, and season it with salt and pepper. Place both on a baking tray, together, and wrap with foil. Cook in the oven for 15 to 20 minutes or until they are both soft. In a small sauce pot, melt the 1 pound of butter. Now, let's plate.

plating

The idea is to create your own individual lobster bake. On each plate, place a serving of potatoes, a few asparagus spears, a corn on the cob, a pinch of each of the herbs, and a small cup of the melted, or drawn, butter. Return the lobsters to the lobster water for 1 minute, remove them after, and set on the plates. You are ready to serve. Make sure you have those fun plastic bibs with little lobsters on them and lobster crackers so people can get to it. I enjoy the warm and moist towelette, as it will get messy, but as mentioned in previous recipes, it is totally worth it!

grilled prawn salad

with mango, Napa cabbage, mint, basil, cucumber, and coconut vinaigrette

---

serves 4

coconut vinaigrette

3 fluid ounces coconut milk

Juice of 2 limes

Zest of 2 limes

1 fluid ounce champagne vinegar

2 Tablespoons extra-virgin olive oil

1 Tablespoon Dijon mustard

½ teaspoon cayenne pepper

1 teaspoon ground coriander

1 pinch salt

grilled prawn salad with mango, Napa cabbage, mint, basil, and cucumber

1½ pounds gulf prawns, 16/20 size, peeled, deveined

2 fluid ounces cooking oil

Salt and pepper, as desired

4 cups Napa cabbage, thinly shaved

1 ripe mango, peeled, sliced

2 cups English cucumber, peeled, seeds removed, ribboned

1 cup basil leaves, destemmed, torn into pieces

1 cup mint leaves, destemmed, torn into pieces

½ cup cilantro leaves, destemmed, roughly chopped

---

what to drink

- Gewürztraminer
- Viognier
- Lager
- Mango daiquiri

what to ask the fish guy

Ask if the lobsters are from Maine or at least the same New England coast. They are the best. If they only have spiny lobsters, that's okay too, but don't expect any claws. If they are willing to steam them for you, do it; it's a lot less hassle and mess. Just remember to tell them you will warm them up later, so a lighter steaming is preferred.

method: coconut vinaigrette

In a blender, combine the coconut milk, lime juice, lime zest, vinegar, olive oil, mustard, cayenne pepper, ground coriander, and a pinch of salt. Reserve for later.

method: grilled prawn salad with mango, Napa cabbage, mint, basil, and cucumber

Start the grill on its highest heat. Scrape and brush it well, and generously oil it; this should always be done before and after each use. Toss the prawns in the cooking oil, and season lightly with salt and pepper. Place prawns on the grill and cook for 2 to 3 minutes on each side. Place on a platter and allow to cool at room temperature. Now, in a mixing bowl add the cabbage, mango, cucumber, basil, mint, and cilantro. Generously mix with the vinaigrette, and reserve some for plating.

plating

Place the dressed salad on a plate, and place the prawns on top. Drizzle a bit of the remaining vinaigrette over the prawns and around the salad, and serve.

dungeness crab rolls

on hot dog buns with lemon and fried pickles

---

serves 4

6 fluid ounces cooking oil

2 kosher pickles, sliced

2 cups flour

2 eggs, beaten

2 cups bread crumbs

Salt and pepper, as desired

1½ pounds crab meat

Juice of 4 lemons

½ cup chives, small diced

8 hot dog buns

Zest of 4 lemons

---

what to drink

- Pinot gris
- Rosé from Provence
- California IPA
- Botanical gin margarita, rocks, no salt

what to ask the fish guy

Ask if the crab meat was picked clean and shells removed. If they don't have Dungeness crab, Jonah is a great substitution. If that is also not a possibility, blue crab is pretty good too.

method

Set a deep pan on the stove and fill it with the cooking oil. Dry the sliced pickles and on a towel and dredge them in the flour; pat off any excess. Place them in the beaten eggs, and transfer them to the bread crumbs, making sure they are evenly coated. Turn the heat to high and when the oil begins to smoke, add in the breaded pickles. Cook for 1 to 2 minutes or until they are golden brown. Remove from the oil and set on paper towels to absorb any excess. Lightly season with salt and pepper, and reserve for plating. Mix the crab meat in a separate bowl with the lemon juice and chives. Do not season with salt, as it doesn't need it. Lightly toast the hot dog buns, and fill with the crab equally. Sprinkle a bit of lemon zest over the top, and that's it!

plating

Put the rolls on each plate. You can either stick the fried pickles in the buns, or serve them on the side.

shrimp and coconut soup

with basil, ginger, and roasted cremini mushroom

serves 4

2 fluid ounces cooking oil

1 medium yellow onion, minced

1 leek, white part only, diced

2 whole shallots, peeled, minced

2 Tablespoons fresh ginger, grated

½ cup lemongrass, finely chopped

2 Tablespoons unsalted butter

2 cups white wine

4 cups unsweetened coconut milk

Juice of 3 limes

Juice of 1 lemon

½ cup jasmine rice

Zest of 1 lemon

Zest of 3 limes

Salt and pepper, as desired

2 cups cremini mushrooms, stems
removed, cut into wedges

1 pound Oregon pink shrimp, cooked

1 cup of basil leaves, destemmed,
torn into pieces

½ cup parsley leaves, destemmed,
roughly chopped

what to drink

- Gewürztraminer
- Viognier
- Lager
- Sake martini

what to ask the fish guy

These little shrimp appear in markets all over the world. The best and most sustainable come from Oregon and Northern California. If the shrimp are from somewhere else and the fish guys are willing, ask to try one. If you don't like it, choose a different garnish.

method

Place a tall pot on the stove over high heat and add the cooking oil. When the oil begins to smoke, add the onion, leek, shallots, ginger, and lemongrass. Turn the heat to low and add the butter. Stir with a wooden spoon every few seconds. Cook for 5 minutes and add the wine. Cook for 3 minutes and add the coconut milk, lime juice, and lemon juice. Reduce the heat to a simmer and cook for 20 minutes. Add the rice, and cook for 10 to 12 more minutes or until the rice is soft. In a blender, and using a towel to hold the top when puréeing, blend the soup and return the contents to the pot. Add the lemon and lime zest, and adjust the seasoning with salt and pepper.

In a frying pan, add enough cooking oil to cover the bottom of the pan and place over a high heat. Add the mushrooms and move them about in the pan. Cook for 2 to 3 minutes and remove the pan from the heat. Season lightly with salt and pepper.

plating

Place a small pile of the pink shrimp in the center of the bowl. Next, add the pan-roasted mushrooms. Pour the hot soup over them. Sprinkle the basil and parsley over the surface of the soup and serve.

grilled halibut

with sweet corn stew, pea tendrils, and tomato vinaigrette

serves 4

tomato vinaigrette

4 ripe roma tomatoes, destemmed, roughly chopped

1 whole shallot, peeled, roughly chopped

1 cup extra-virgin olive oil

½ cup sherry vinegar

1 teaspoon tomato paste

1 Tablespoon Dijon mustard

Salt and pepper, as desired

½ cup parsley leaves, destemmed, roughly chopped

grilled halibut with sweet corn stew and pea tendrils

2 fluid ounces cooking oil

½ cup red onion, peeled, small diced

1 red bell pepper, destemmed, deseeded, small diced

2 cups raw corn, cut from the cob

2 fluid ounces white wine

1 cup heavy cream

Juice of 1 lemon

1 Tablespoon prepared roasted garlic

Zest of 1 lemon

1 teaspoon cornstarch

2 teaspoons water

1 Tablespoon whole oregano leaves, destemmed

Salt and pepper, as desired

4 (5–6-ounce) pieces of halibut filet, skin off

¼ pound pea tendrils

what to drink

- Rosé champagne
- Bandol rosé
- Red ale
- Tom Collins

what to ask the fish guy

Ask for Alaskan halibut; it is the most sustainable and yields the highest amount. Have her or him cut you 5-ounce portions, and ask for the skin to be removed.

method: tomato vinaigrette

In a blender, combine the tomatoes, shallot, extra-virgin olive oil, vinegar, tomato paste, mustard, and a pinch of salt. Mix until smooth and then transfer to a small sauce pot. Set over a medium heat and simmer for 15 minutes. Add parsley and adjust seasoning with salt and pepper as desired. Set aside for later.

method: grilled halibut with sweet corn stew and pea tendrils

In a sauce pot, bring 1 fluid ounce of cooking oil to its smoking point and add the red onion, red bell pepper, and corn. Cook for 2 to 3 minutes, stirring regularly. Add the white wine and cook until the pot is almost dry. Then, add the cream, lemon juice, roasted garlic, and lemon zest. Cook for 3 minutes. Mix the cornstarch and water together. Stir this mixture into the corn and cook for 5 minutes. Stir in the oregano leaves and adjust seasoning with salt and pepper as desired. Leave this in the pot for later.

Grill the halibut, moving it regularly to create an even charring. Grill on one side for 5 minutes and turn using a fish spatula or small metal spatula. Cook for another 3 to 4 minutes, checking regularly for doneness. Cooking halibut slightly undercooked is the best, as it can be eaten raw. If cooked to medium, it retains its moisture and optimal flavor.

plating

Heat the corn and vinaigrette gently. Place a spoonful of sweet corn stew in a bowl. In the center, put a small pile of pea tendrils, and then place the cooked halibut on top. Drizzle a few spoonfuls of vinaigrette on and around the fish. Serve immediately.

pan-fried petrale sole

with raw heirloom tomato sauce, torn basil, and caper berries

---

serves 4

raw heirloom tomato sauce

2 cups heirloom tomatoes, stems removed, roughly chopped

1 cup extra-virgin olive oil

1 whole shallot, peeled, roughly cut

1 cup pasilla pepper, destemmed, deseeded, roughly chopped

½ cup red wine vinegar

Salt and pepper, as desired

pan-fried petrale sole with torn basil and caper berries

4 Tablespoons all-purpose flour

2 fluid ounces water

½ cup cornstarch

1 Tablespoon baking powder

1 egg, beaten

1 pinch salt

4 fluid ounces cooking oil

I whole petrale sole, pan-ready

1 cup basil leaves, destemmed, torn into pieces

½ cup caper berries, destemmed, halved lengthwise

---

what to drink

- Rosé cava from Spain
- Chianti classico
- Red ale
- Aromatic gin gibson

what to ask the fish guy

Ask that they have been cleaned and are pan-ready; they just have to make a small cut by the gills and scoop out the stuff that you do not want in your garbage can. Ask that they scale the fish, give it a gentle rinse, and score it so that it ultimately cooks evenly.

method: raw heirloom tomato sauce

In a food processor or blender, combine the chopped tomatoes, olive oil, shallots, pasilla peppers, and red wine vinegar. Mix for 1 minute, leaving it still a bit chunky. Adjust seasoning with salt and pepper as desired. Reserve at room temperature for later.

method: pan-fried petrale sole with torn basil and caper berries

We'll begin by making a tempura-like batter. Combine the water, flour, cornstarch, baking powder, egg, and a pinch of salt in a mixing bowl. Whisk until smooth. It should resemble pancake batter. If it is too thick, add another tablespoon of water. Set a pan on the stove with the cooking oil and heat this on high. When the oil begins to smoke, quickly dip the petrale sole in the batter and carefully place in the hot oil. Turn the heat down to medium and cook them for 5 minutes. If they aren't submerged, flip them over after 3 minutes. Transfer them to a plate with paper towels to absorb any excess oil.

plating

Place an even coating of the raw and room temperature tomato sauce on the plate. Set the fried sole on top, and sprinkle the basil leaf pieces and caper berries around the plate. That's it.

baked local sole

with shaved zucchini and olive salad and roasted red pepper coulis

serves 4

roasted red pepper coulis

2 red bell peppers, roasted, skin and
    seeds removed

2 Tablespoons extra-virgin olive oil

2 Tablespoons water

1 Tablespoon balsamic vinegar

baked local sole with shaved zucchini and olive salad

2 zucchinis, ribboned

1 cup green olives, pitted, cut into
    ¼-inch pieces

1 Tablespoon prepared roasted garlic

1 cup cherry tomatoes, halved

1 Tablespoon champagne vinegar

Juice of 1 lemon

Zest of 1 lemon

1 Tablespoon chives, small diced

1 Tablespoon oregano leaves,
    destemmed, roughly chopped

Salt and pepper, as desired

2 (2½–3-pound) whole local sole filets

what to drink

- California sparkling wine
- Rosé from Provence
- Lager
- A cocktail of cachaça and
  muddled red bell pepper, citrus,
  and basil served on the rocks

what to ask the fish guy

Ask for whole fish, around 2 pounds each. Then, ask them to make a gentle slice on the skin down the middle of each side and also along the 4 exterior curves along the fins; this makes removing the skin after baking less arduous of a task.

method: roasted red pepper coulis

In a blender, add the cleaned roasted red bell peppers, olive oil, water, and balsamic vinegar and mix until smooth. Adjust seasoning with salt and pepper and set aside at room temperature.

method: baked local sole with shaved zucchini and olive salad

Combine the shaved zucchini, olives, roasted garlic, tomatoes, vinegar, and lemon juice in a mixing bowl and let stand for 10 minutes. Add the lemon zest, chives, and oregano. Season with only a pinch of pepper; the olives are salty and will do the trick. Set this aside for plating.

Preheat your oven to 450°F. Place the sole on a baking sheet lined with wax or parchment paper. Rub them with cooking oil and generously season both sides with salt and pepper. Bake the sole for 12 to 15 minutes or until they are cooked through. Let them rest for 2 minutes and peel the skin off. Using your spatula, you should now be able to easily lift the filets off the sheet. Let's plate!

plating

Place a good amount of the zucchini salad in the middle of the plate. Lay the filet of sole on top. Spoon some red bell pepper coulis on the side of the plate and serve immediately.

pan-seared tru cod

with salted cantaloupe, sweet corn, cherry tomato, verbena, and oregano

---

serves 4

2 cups cantaloupe, peeled, seeds removed, cut into chunks, sprinkled with a little salt

1 cup fresh or thawed frozen corn

1 cup cherry tomatoes, halved

2 Tablespoons lemon verbena, sliced

¼ cup Thai basil leaves, destemmed, torn into pieces

2 Tablespoons oregano leaves, roughly chopped

3 Tablespoons extra-virgin olive oil

Salt and pepper, as desired

4 (5-ounce) tru cod filets, skin on

2 fluid ounces cooking oil

what to drink

- Aligoté
- Chinon rosé
- Summer ale
- Dark 'n stormy

what to ask the fish guy

Ask for the thicker side of the cod loin, and let them know you want the portions to be 5 ounces each. Although it might sound like you are asking a lot, ask them to leave the skin on and slightly score the skin down the middle. This shouldn't be a problem as they have the knives and they are cutting this for you anyway. By scoring the skin, the fish will cook more evenly as the skin will stay in the cooking oil throughout the process. If not, there is a good possibility that the fish will buckle or curve away from the oil, leaving the center uncooked.

method

Mix everything except for the cod in a mixing bowl and adjust the seasoning with salt and pepper as desired. Set aside for later. In a medium-sized frying pan, add the cooking oil and set over high heat. Pat the skin of the cod dry with a paper towel and season with an even sprinkling of salt and pepper. The patting-dry step will prevent the fish from sticking to the pan. Once the oil in the pan begins to smoke, place the fish gently in the pan with the skin side down. Let the fish cook for 30 seconds and lower the heat to medium. Cook them for 1 minute, and using a fish spatula or a thin metal spatula, lift the fish and move them slightly to ensure the skin is not sticking to the pan. Add the teaspoon of butter to the pan and cook for 2 more minutes. Turn the cod over onto the opposite side, and cook for 3 to 4 minutes. Check them every 30 seconds and cook until the fish is firm; if you want to peek inside, do it! The fish should be opaque and set firmly. Serve immediately.

plating

Set the garnish in the center of the plate and the fish on top. Using the liquid from the original bowl with the garnish, drizzle that over the fish and around the plate. You are all set.

the cod melt

with sharp cheddar, dijon, grilled local cod, and brioche

serves 4

4 (4-ounce) cod filets, skin off

8 (1-inch thick) slices of brioche
    bread loaf

2 Tablespoons Dijon mustard

8 slices sharp cheddar

1 cup wild arugula

what to drink

- White vin de savoie
- Pinot Blanc
- Farmhouse ale
- Amaretto sour

what to ask the fish guy

Ask for four 4-ounce pieces of cod with the skin off. Ask them to show you the vertebrae side of the filet and remember to put that side down on the grill first when grilling.

method

Fire up the grill. Scrape it, brush it, and generously oil it. Rub oil on the cod filets and season them lightly with salt and pepper. Place them on the grill and cook them on the first side for 3 to 4 minutes. Move them regularly to prevent burning. Turn them over and repeat the process for 3 to 4 more minutes or until the fish is cooked through. Remove from heat and assemble the sandwiches.

    Lay the sliced brioche out in two rows of four, and lightly but evenly spread the mustard on the bread. Next, place a slice of cheddar on each piece of bread, and then place the fish on four of the slices.

    Add the arugula if you wish (you could add bacon, tomato, or whatever else you like in a melt). Close the sandwiches. If you have a panini press, fire it up! If you are more of a traditionalist, set a large frying pan on the stove with enough cooking oil to coat the bottom of the pan. Turn the heat to medium and preheat the pan. Add the assembled sandwiches to the pan, and toast lightly on each side, regularly flipping to evenly color and melt the cheese. Remove from the pan to a cutting board.

plating

Once the sandwiches are sitting on the cutting board, slice them in half. Serve immediately before they cool off.

grilled wild king salmon

with cherry tomato, sweet corn, crushed cucumbers, and oregano

serves 4

1½ cups English cucumbers, peeled, deseeded, cut into chunks

3 Tablespoons extra-virgin olive oil

1 Tablespoon champagne vinegar

1 Tablespoon cracked black pepper

Juice of 1 lemon

Zest of 1 lemon

1 cup cherry tomatoes, halved

1 cup fresh cooked or thawed frozen sweet corn

1 Tablespoon oregano leaves, destemmed, roughly chopped

1 Tablespoon thyme leaves, destemmed

2 fluid ounces cooking oil

4 (5-ounce) wild king salmon filets, skin on

Salt and pepper, as desired

what to drink

- Pigato
- Anderson valley rosé
- Brown ale
- Whiskey sour

what to ask the fish guy

Ask for four 5-ounce portions of wild king salmon. The Pacific salmon is viewed as a more sustainable choice, but be sure to avoid all farm-raised products. Ask that the fish is scaled, skin left on, and pin bones removed. You will want to check again when you are setting your kitchen that they pulled out all the little pin bones. If you feel one while gently moving your finger over the filet, you can easily wiggle it out using a pair of needle-nose pliers.

method

Fire up the grill. Scrape it, brush it, and oil it generously; you don't want your last grilled meal ending up on the fish, and fish stick to the grill quite easily. In a mixing bowl, add the cucumbers, extra-virgin olive oil, vinegar, black pepper, lemon juice and zest, and crush with a wooden spoon. Now, add the tomatoes, corn, oregano, and thyme. Set this aside for plating.

Rub the fish with the cooking oil all over and season lightly with salt and pepper. Place the skin side on the grill and cook for 30 to 45 seconds. At this point, move the fish around every 30 seconds to avoid burning the skin and to evenly cook it. Watch as the filet side also begins to cook. You'll continue cooking on the skin for 6 to 8 minutes, and then flip the filet over and cook for 2 to 3 more minutes or until it is medium. Remove from the grill. Let's plate.

plating

Set the veggies in the center of the plate and pour some of the juices over them. Place the portion of grilled salmon on top, and you are ready to roll.

smoked trout salad

with summer herbs and mojito vinaigrette

serves 4

mojito vinaigrette

½ cup grapeseed oil

2 Tablespoons light rum

Juice of 1 lime

Zest of 1 lime

1 Tablespoon champagne vinegar

1 teaspoon Dijon mustard

1 whole shallot, peeled and minced

Salt and pepper, as desired

smoked trout salad with summer herbs

1 cup fresh parsley leaves, destemmed, roughly chopped

½ cup whole marjoram leaves, destemmed

½ cup chives, roughly cut

¼ pound wild arugula

12 ounces smoked trout

what to drink

- Sauvignon blanc
- Gruener Vetliner
- White ale
- Mojito

method: mojito vinaigrette

In a blender, mix the grapeseed oil, rum, lime juice and zest, vinegar, mustard, and shallot for 1 minute or until smooth. Check the seasoning and adjust with salt and pepper. Reserve for later.

method: smoked trout salad with summer herbs

Pick through the herbs and arugula and discard any wilted pieces. Place in a mixing bowl. Flake the smoked trout into small chunks and add them to the mixing bowl. Add the herbs and half of the dressing. Taste and add more dressing, salt, and pepper as desired.

plating

This is essentially ready to go, so mix it one last time so everything is even, and plate as you would a basic green salad. Serve away.

131

salmon burgers

with heirloom tomato, sweet gem lettuce, and creole mustard

serves 4

1½ pounds wild king salmon filets, skin off

½ cup bread crumbs

2 eggs

2 Tablespoons soy sauce

1 Tablespoon Worcestershire sauce

1 Tablespoon parsley leaves, destemmed, roughly chopped

1 bunch scallions, thinly sliced

Salt and pepper, as desired

4 burger buns

2 Tablespoons creole mustard

8 sweet gem lettuce leaves*

1 large heirloom tomato, sliced into ¼-inch thick wheels

what to drink
- Tocai friulano
- Beaujolais
- Gose
- Mint julep

what to ask the fish guy

Ask them to make sure it is wild king salmon. Next, ask that all the pin bones and skin be removed, and any cartilage be cut off; this is the tricky part. It's a big ask, but see if they will mince it for you, as mentioned earlier. It won't kill you to ask, and worst case scenario, you do it yourself! The good news is that it is easy; I'm just trying to save you a bit of time and cleaning.

method

If you managed to get the fish guy to chop up the salmon for you, then I am impressed. If not, I'm not surprised, so get that fish on a cutting board and start chopping it into "burger" meat. Once it is all chopped, transfer it over to a mixing bowl and refrigerate for 15 minutes. Next, add the bread crumbs, eggs, soy sauce, Worcestershire sauce, parsley, scallions, and a pinch of salt and pepper. Mix well and refrigerate again for 15 minutes. While that's happening, fire up the grill. Scape it, brush it, and oil it generously—you may have heard this before. Now, let's form the salmon patties. Divide the mix into four equal parts, and ball them up as if you were making snowballs . . . or burgers. Oil them well, and place on the grill. Let them cook for 1 minute, and begin moving them around every 10 to 15 seconds to avoid burning. Cook them this way on each side for 3 to 5 minutes. Remove from the grill, and quickly toast the burger buns on the grill.

plating

Evenly spread the creole mustard on both sides of the buns. Place the salmon burger on the bottom bun, top with a couple slices each of lettuce and tomato, and it's a burger!

*Baby romaine or torn romaine leaves are a great substitution.

the timeless tuna tartare

with pineapple, cucumber, soy sauce, cilantro, and sesame crackers

serves 4

1 pound #1 or #1+ sashimi grade
   yellowfin ahi tuna, cubed

½ cup fresh pineapple, peeled,
   minced

½ cup red onion, peeled, minced

½ cup cucumber, peeled, deseeded,
   finely diced

1 ripe avocado, peeled, pit removed,
   diced

3 Tablespoons soy sauce

1 Tablespoon sesame oil

1 Tablespoon extra-virgin olive oil

Zest of 1 lime

Juice of 1 lime

½ cup cilantro leaves, destemmed,
   roughly chopped

½ cup mint leaves, destemmed,
   roughly chopped

1 box sesame crackers

what to drink

- Cold sake
- Gewürztraminer
- Japanese lager
- Rum punch

what to ask the fish guy

Ask if they have #1 or #1+ grade tuna. #2+ is fine but usually has more waste.

Next, make sure it is handline caught. Hawaiian longline and free school are reasonable second choices, but avoid the troll caught stuff.

Ask them to remove the skin and bloodline for you as well. This will leave you with a ready to dice product.

If they are not too busy and you seem to be getting along, you could even ask that they dice it for you in ½-inch cubes. Good luck!

method

I suppose it's reasonable if the fish professional didn't want to dice the fish for you. Next time, try bribing them with beer. This means that you have to cut it yourself, so ¼-inch cubes are the most pleasant to eat. Cut the tuna and place the cubes in a mixing bowl. Now, add everything else except for the crackers. Mix it very well and adjust the seasoning with salt and pepper. If you would prefer more sesame, soy sauce, or lime, go ahead and cautiously add that which you seek. Cooking is subjective, and I really love this recipe because it still works well regardless of how everything is balanced. Please remember that you can always add but you cannot take away, so when tweaking to your own preference, caution is recommended.

plating

Place the tuna tartare in a bowl. Place the crackers in a bowl next to it. That's it!

sweet corn and blueberry pound cake

with strawberry salsa and strawberry basil sauce

serves 6

strawberry basil sauce

1 cup strawberries, stems removed, cut into ¼-inch pieces

½ cup water

1 teaspoon honey

½ cup basil leaves

sweet corn and blueberry pound cake

2 Tablespoons + 1 cup unsalted butter, softened to room temperature

3 cups all-purpose flour

3 cups + 1 pinch granulated sugar

1 teaspoon salt

1 teaspoon baking powder

Zest of 1 lemon

5 eggs

1 cup buttermilk

1 cup sweet corn, kernels pan roasted and set aside to cool

1 cup blueberries

1 cup strawberries, stems removed, cut into ¼-inch pieces

1 lime, peeled, segments cut out, diced

what to drink

- Moscato d'Asti
- Brochette d' Acqui
- Lambic
- Irish coffee

what to ask the fish guy

Hope you are having a nice day?

method: strawberry basil sauce

In a blender, combine 1 cup of strawberries, the water, honey, and basil. Purée this until smooth and set aside for plating.

method: sweet corn and blueberry pound cake

Preheat your oven to 350°F and grease a small loaf pan or 9-inch baking pan well with the 2 tablespoons of butter. In a mixing bowl, combine flour, sugar, salt, baking powder, and lemon zest. Mix them together well. In a separate bowl, or with an electric mixer using the paddle attachment, mix the 1 cup of butter and eggs. Once fully mixed, add the buttermilk and fold together with the flour mixture. Next, fold in the corn and blueberries, and pour this batter into a small loaf pan or 9-inch cake pan, the same one you greased a moment ago. Bake for 40 to 50 minutes. When the cake pulls away from the sides, and when you can stick a fork in it and it comes out clean, you're done. Let cool while you prepare the two other components. In a small mixing bowl, add the other cup of strawberries. Mix with lime segments and season with a pinch of granulated sugar.

plating

Cut a piece of cake and set on plate. Spoon some sauce on the side and around the cake. Top with a small amount of strawberry salsa and serve.

FALL

barbecued oysters
with cayenne-kissed cucumber salsa / 143

steamed manila clams
with fennel, grapefruit, apple, and
tarragon / 144

bay scallop fish tacos
with cilantro, pineapple, crème fraîche, and
corn tortillas / 147

beer-steamed mussels
with sausage, apple, garlic, and thyme / 148

whole roasted dungeness crab
with roasted potatoes, lemons, hot salty
butter, and grilled artichokes / 151

pan-roasted prawns
with fettuccini, mild blue cheese, brandy,
and sage / 152

lobster mac 'n cheese
with bread crumbs, tarragon, and
lemon / 155

rock shrimp po' boy
with lettuce, tomato, and
creole remoulade / 156

sautéed fluke
with grilled scallions, poached egg, and
caviar cream / 159

grilled halibut
with curried apples, pineapple, mint,
sunflower seeds, and avocado / 160

grilled day-boat scallops
with roasted cauliflower, shishito peppers,
and heirloom tomato salsa / 163

pan-roasted rock cod
with blood orange, baby beets, brussels
sprouts, and horseradish vinaigrette / 165

grilled albacore
with pretzel spoon bread, roasted squash,
and carrot ginger sauce / 167

smoked sockeye salmon
with quick spice bread, cardamom cream,
and garlic cucumbers / 171

seared yellowfin tuna
with toasted pumpkin seeds, chestnut
butter, pear, fennel, and grapefruit / 172

tuna sashimi
with grilled apple salsa, mint leaves, toasted
sesame, and mustard seed oil / 175

sweet potato and ginger tarte
with cinnamon pear sauce and angel food
cake croutons / 176

whole roasted fish taco bar
with guacamole, salsa, grated cheese, lime,
and cilantro leaves / 179

the final fish tale

this one is about the prawn in london that taught me how to love the experience of dining

Puberty is mean. Albeit a rite of passage, and even though great parents can guide their kids through it, one cannot deny the inherent evil that is puberty. My parents are actually wonderful people that tolerated this from me and my three siblings. During my hormonal El Niño, we moved to London, England where I attended eighth grade.

So, puberty is mean. We covered this. But there was something excellent about being a boy in the northwest of London circa the Reagan administration. There once stood an epic establishment run by an Italian couple only a few blocks past the fabled Abbey Road Studio, and from our apartment, you could see the tourists take photos mimicking the Beatles' Abbey Road album cover . . . I wonder if that still happens in today's digital age? A few blocks past stood a pub that taught me to love beer. They saw the man that I would be rather than the boy I was, so they served me these delicious ales a handful of years before they should have (but you had to love their insight). With a shaky voice, a lot of unwelcomed hair, not a friend in sight, and being a teenage food lover in

search of pretty much anything that would make life better and less dramatic, my parents found it. You needed to go a few blocks past the pub and take a soft left, and there you were.

Fontana Amorosa, the fountain of love, and the first time I was romanced by a happily married woman. She was the wife and maître d', and her husband was the chef. I would ultimately be known as Casanova as we frequented as a family thereafter (my little brother who, back then, was just a puppy with glasses, would be known as *professore*). We laughed, we ate, my parents drank the amazing wines, but I was intoxicated by the experience. We were part of it. They remembered us, gave us nicknames, and remembered that I had to have the *gamberi all'aglio*, or prawns with garlic. It was sublime. My pubescent taste buds simply couldn't select another menu item—that was it!

Prawns and shrimp are everywhere, they are mild and delicious, but that little spot in London's northwest serves as a great example of how a prolific and easily sourced fish, simply cooked to greatness, can curl your toes and leave a lasting memory.

barbecued oysters

with cayenne-kissed cucumber salsa

---

serves 4

cayenne-kissed cucumber salsa

Juice of 1 lemon

1 Tablespoon sliced basil leaves

1 Tablespoon red onion, small diced

1 Tablespoon extra-virgin olive oil

¼ tsp cayenne pepper

2 cucumbers, peeled, seeds removed, minced

barbecued oysters

24 local oysters, shucked, sliced away from shell, placed back in shell

---

what to drink

- Moscato
- Arneis
- Pilsner
- Tequila gimlet

what to ask the fish guy

Ask when the oysters were harvested. By law, they must keep shellfish tags on hand, so they should be able to assist. If the harvest date is more than five days ago, don't buy them. This doesn't mean they are necessarily bad, but the quality may be lesser. Unless you are visiting an oyster farm in Marshall, California, the likelihood of getting same-day oysters is slim. Up to four days is normally fine.

method: cayenne-kissed cucumber salsa

Combine all ingredients, apart from the oysters and cucumbers, in a blender and purée. Mix in with minced cucumbers. Adjust seasoning with salt, lemon juice, and desired amount of cayenne pepper.

method: barbecued oysters

Wash the oysters in cold water, scrubbing well to remove all dirt and sand. Fire up the grill; the hotter the better. Use a proper oyster knife to gently pry them open at the thickest part of the shell (you will see what appears to be a sort of hinge). Remember that finesse is key in not breaking the shell and getting pieces of shell in the dish. Using the same oyster knife, cut the attached part of the oyster away from the deeper side of the oyster; leave the oyster in the shell. Once the salsa is ready, place the oysters on the grill, shell side down so you can watch as the oyster gently curls as it cooks. This usually takes about 2 minutes.

plating

Once the oysters have curled a bit they are ready. Top each one with some cucumber salsa and serve immediately.

steamed manila clams

with fennel, grapefruit, apple, and tarragon

serves 4

2 pounds manila clams

2 fluid ounces cooking oil

1 cup fennel, diced

2 whole shallots, peeled, sliced

2 Tablespoons unsalted butter

Salt, as desired

1 bottle white wine

1 Tablespoon cracked black pepper

Juice of 1 lemon

Zest of 1 lemon

½ cup ripe apple, peeled, core
    removed, diced

2 Tablespoons tarragon, leaves
    plucked from stems, and roughly
    chopped

½ cup grapefruit, peeled, segments
    removed

what to drink

- Chardonnay
- Pinot gris
- California IPA
- Salty dog

what to ask the fish guy

With all shellfish, my first question is "when was this harvested?" I usually give them a reasonable max of five days—if older than that, don't buy them.

method

Place clams in a bowl and sit beneath cold running water; let them sit there for 10 minutes, then move them around to try and get rid of any sand that may still possibly be present. Heat the cooking oil in a pot. When you see it about to smoke, add the fennel and shallots. Immediately remove the pan from the heat and add the butter. Add a pinch of salt, and stir the ingredients in the pot. Return the pan to the heat, keeping it on medium, and continue to stir until the fennel and shallots have softened. Now, add the clams to the pot and stir for 30 seconds. Pour the wine into the pot and keep on a medium heat. This next part is critical. You must stand over the pot and watch as the clams begin to open. The moment they open is when they must be removed from the pot. Have a separate bowl, ultimately the serving bowl, close by to pluck them from the pot and place in this bowl. You will have the occasional clam that doesn't open. Throw those guys away. Once the clams are out of the pot and in the bowl, add the pepper, lemon juice, lemon zest, diced apples, tarragon, and grapefruit pieces.

plating

Place the desired number of clams in each bowl and pour the broth over them. What you do now is up to you; you could refer back to winter and find another clam recipe and make some garlic bread, you could get some fresh bread for dunking, or you can eat these sweet little guys by themselves and the broth as a soup. Remember to have a separate bowl to discard the shells.

bay scallop fish tacos

with cilantro, pineapple, crème fraîche, and corn tortillas

serves 4

1 pound bay scallops, shucked

2 fluid ounces cooking oil

1 Tablespoon unsalted butter

Salt and pepper, as desired

12 corn tortillas, grilled or quickly toasted on the exposed burner of the stove until soft

1 cup crème fraîche

1 cup of savoy cabbage, thinly shaved

1 cup pineapple, peeled, small diced

1 cup of cilantro leaves, destemmed

Juice of 1 lime

Zest of 1 lime

what to drink

- Albariño
- Vinho verde
- A light lager
- Margarita on the rocks, no salt

what to ask the fish guy

Not much to do here. The Nantucket bay scallops are without question the finest of them all. Start there.

And always ask the question of freshness and when they were harvested. The more recent the better.

method

Lay the scallops out on a tray, and using a towel, pat them dry of any excess moisture. Set a large frying pan over a high heat and coat the bottom with the cooking oil. When the pan begins to smoke, add the scallops and pull the pan off of the heat. Shake the pan around quickly, and immediately add the butter. Return to high heat and cook for 45 seconds. Remove the scallops from the pan and sprinkle them with a small amount of salt and pepper. Lay out the tortillas on a cutting board, and smear some crème fraîche inside. Place some shaved cabbage next, followed by pineapple cubes and cilantro leaves. Place the scallops on top, and sprinkle each with some lime juice and lime zest.

plating

It is best to serve them laying open and flat so when the person eating them is ready, they can make the typical taco fold. If you are going for a certain look and want to fold them, a bamboo skewer to pierce them closed at the top works; just go at an angle.

beer-steamed mussels

with sausage, apple, garlic, and thyme

___

serves 4

2 fluid ounces cooking oil

2 links sweet sausage, cooked, cut
  into ½-inch thick disc-shaped
  pieces

2 whole shallots, peeled, sliced

1 Tablespoon butter

3 cloves garlic, peeled, halved
  lengthwise, sprout removed,
  sliced

2 Tablespoons thyme leaves,
  destemmed

2 dark beers, red or brown ales

2 pounds mussels, cleaned

1 cup Granny Smith apple, peeled,
  core removed, cut into small
  chunks

Juice of 1 lemon

Zest of 1 lemon

Salt and pepper, as desired

Fresh bread, optional

___

what to drink

- German Riesling
- Belgian triple

what to ask the fish guy

Ask for PEI (Prince Edward Island) Mussels. To be honest, I lived with a few Canadians once upon a time, and I found them uncomfortably kind and annoyingly more organized, politically—but their mussels are the best. If you have willing fishmongers in front of you, ask if they are willing to debeard the mussels for you. The stringy little hairs that peek out of the mussel are inedible and referred to as the beard (technically, byssal threads, which allow them to attach to their surroundings). If the fishmongers won't debeard them for you, ask them to show you how. You need to wash each mussel, as they can be sandy, and then you need to grab those little fibers peeking out and gently wiggle them out.

method

In a large pot, add the cooking oil. When the oil begins to smoke, add the sausage pieces. Cook for 2 minutes, then add the shallots, butter, sliced garlic, and thyme. Now, add the beer. Let it simmer for 2 minutes and add the mussels. Bring to a boil and add the apple, lemon juice, and lemon zest. Stand by the mussels and remove them one by one as they open. Once the mussels are in a serving bowl, adjust the seasoning with salt and pepper as desired, and pour all of the contents back into the bowl.

plating

At this point, having a discard bowl for the mussel shells is a great idea. Serve the big bowl of mussels to the table, some fresh bread for dunking, if you wish, and enjoy.

whole roasted dungeness crab

with roasted potatoes, lemons, hot salty butter, and grilled artichokes

---

serves 4

1 pound fingerling potatoes, halved lengthwise

3 fluid ounces cooking oil

2 cloves fresh garlic, peeled, crushed

1 Tablespoon thyme leaves, destemmed

Salt and pepper, as desired

4 whole artichokes or 2 cups jarred artichoke hearts, sliced

1 cup extra-virgin olive oil

Juice of 1 lemon

2 (2-pound) whole crabs, cooked

½ pound lightly salted butter, slowly melted

2 lemons, quartered lengthwise

---

what to drink

- Red ale
- Brut champagne
- Pigato from Liguria
- Cynar Negroni

what to ask the fish guy

Ask for cooked crabs; they usually have some. Ask them to crack them for you; this will save you a lot of time and help avoid the mess.

method

Preheat your oven to 400°F. Place the cut potatoes in a pot of cold water and bring to a boil. Once they reach a boil, lower heat to a simmer and cook for 1 minute. Strain and allow them to cool. Next, toss them in 1 ounce of cooking oil and spread them out evenly on a baking tray. Place them in the oven and cook for 5 to 6 minutes or until they are golden brown. Turn them over to cook evenly, and roast for 5 more minutes; check to make sure the outside is crispy and that they are soft in the center. Then, add the crushed garlic, cook for two minutes, and remove. Sprinkle with the thyme leaves and salt and pepper as desired. Set aside for later.

Turn on the grill. Remove the exterior leaves of the artichoke and halve lengthwise. Cut away the rest of the leaves, and scoop out the fuzzy part or thistle in the middle. Peel the stem, and place in olive oil in a small sauce pot. Over a medium to low heat, simmer until they are tender, approximately 20 minutes. Remove from the oil and cool . . . or just buy the jarred hearts. Either way, toss them in cooking oil with a pinch of salt and a squeeze of lemon juice. Grill them by moving them regularly around to avoid burning them. Cook for 3 minutes and set on the tray with the potatoes for later. Slice and set aside

Ideally, you bought steamed crabs from the fish guy. If you didn't, first set a large pot of water to boil. Quickly drop the crabs in the boiling water, and set a timer for 8 minutes. Carefully remove the crabs from the boiling water and set on a baking tray. Place the tray in the oven, and at the same time, place the tray of potatoes and artichokes in the oven. If you bought cooked crabs, the method begins here. Set a small sauce pot with the butter over medium heat and melt. Keep warm for plating. Roast for 4 to 5 minutes and serve.

plating

Pull the top shell off of the crab by grabbing it from the rear and lifting. Break the crab in half and place on a platter. Place a bowl of butter and everything else on this platter, including the lemon wedges, and make sure there are a few lobster crackers to get claw meat out of the shell!

pan-roasted prawns

with fettuccini, mild blue cheese, brandy, and sage

serves 4

½ pound dry fettuccini pasta or 1
   pound fresh

2 fluid ounces cooking oil

2 pounds gulf prawns, 16/20 size,
   peeled, deveined

Salt and pepper, as desired

2 whole shallots, peeled and sliced

½ cup brandy

1 cup heavy whipping cream

1 cup local and mild blue cheese*

Juice of 1 lemon

Zest of 1 lemon

½ cup sage leaves, destemmed, torn
   into pieces

½ cup parsley leaves, destemmed,
   chopped

what to drink

- Zweigelt
- Chinon or a light Cabernet Franc
- Brown ale
- Single malt scotch

what to ask the fish guy

Make sure you are buying wild gulf prawns from the Gulf of Mexico, preferably skim-net caught. Buy the peeled and deveined product. I love the 16/20 sizing. If you can find it, the U/9's are great (this means that less than 9 make up one pound). Avoid the farm-raised product from Asia. The methods are questionable and flavor is not nearly as delicious.

method

Set a pot of lightly salted water to boil. When it reaches a rolling boil, add the fettuccini. Stir with a wooden spoon every 2 to 3 minutes so the pasta doesn't clump together. It should take approximately 10 minutes until it is cooked; you can double check by removing a piece from the water and taking a bite. If it is still raw or at all crunchy, keep cooking. Strain the pasta and place on a baking tray when it is done cooking. Drizzle 1 fluid ounce of cooking oil and mix the oil evenly with the pasta so it doesn't stick together while it cools.

Now, lightly season the prawns with salt and pepper, and set a large frying pan on the stove over medium heat. Add enough cooking oil to coat the bottom of the pan, and when it begins to smoke, add the prawns. Spread them out evenly and cook for 2 minutes. Turn them over to sear the other side and cook for 30 seconds. Remove the prawns from the pan, temporarily, and return the pan with the fishy oil to the stove. Add the sliced shallots and cook for 2 to 3 minutes or until they are soft. Have the brandy close by. If you have a gas stove, this will get pretty interesting right now. Hold the pan away from the heat and add the brandy. Keep a safe distance from the stove as the alcohol from the brandy will flame up quite aggressively; if you are too close, you may lose your eyebrows. After 30 seconds, return the pan to the stove, and a smaller more manageable flame will appear. When the flame dies down, this means you have cooked the alcohol off and you can add the cream. Cook this for 2 minutes, and then, little by little, whisk in the blue cheese. When it is all whisked in, add the lemon juice, lemon zest, sage, and parsley. Return the prawns to the pan and cook for 3 minutes. Add in the cooked pasta and mix everything together.

plating

Using tongs, divide the pasta equally into bowls, leaving the prawns and some sauce in the pan. Place the prawns around the pasta, dividing equally so that nobody gets upset. Pour the remaining sauce over the pasta and serve.

*Point Reyes Blue in Northern California and Bayley Hazen Blue from Vermont are good options.

lobster mac 'n cheese

with bread crumbs, tarragon, and lemon

serves 4

2 (1½-pound) live Maine lobsters

½ pound elbow macaroni pasta

2 fluid ounces cooking oil

1 Tablespoon yellow onions, minced

2 fluid ounces white wine

2 egg yolks

1 cup + 2 Tablespoons water

2 teaspoons cornstarch

2 cups heavy whipping cream

12 ounces sharp cheddar cheese, grated

1 teaspoon cayenne pepper

2 teaspoons salt

Juice of 1 lemon

Zest of 1 lemon

½ cup tarragon leaves, destemmed, chopped

1 cup panko bread crumbs

what to drink

- Vintage champagne
- Meursault
- Pilsner
- Botanical gin and tonic with a lemon

what to ask the fish guy

Ask if the lobsters are from Maine or at least the same New England coast. They are the best. If they only have spiny lobsters, that's okay too, but don't expect any claws. If they are willing to steam them for you, do it; it's a lot less hassle and mess. Just remember to tell them you will warm them up later, so a lighter steaming is preferred.

method

To begin, set a large pot of unsalted water to boil for the lobsters, and also set a medium-sized pot of lightly salted water to boil for the elbow macaroni. Have a large pair of tongs and a large spoon ready. Now, have a look at the lobsters and make sure the rubber bands are still around their claws—it can be very interesting if they're not. Place them quickly into the unsalted boiling water and use the tongs and spoon to dunk them. Keep a safe distance, as they may flap their tail and splash some hot water on you. Set your timer for 7 minutes. Once the 7 minutes have passed, transfer them to the ice water and let them cool for 10 to 12 minutes. Remove from the ice water, crack the shells, and remove the lobster meat from the shells. Cut into bite-sized chunks and reserve for later. When the water for the pasta is boiling, add the elbow macaroni. Stir every 2 minutes to ensure that it doesn't clump and that it cooks evenly. Cook for 8 minutes and strain. Rinse it well in cold water and toss it with 1 fluid ounce of cooking oil. Set aside for later.

In a medium sauce pan, add the remaining 1 fluid ounce of cooking oil and set over a medium heat. When it begins to smoke, add the onions. Stir with a wooden spoon and let it cook for 2 minutes. Add the wine, and simmer for 3 minutes. In a mixing bowl, whisk the egg yolks, 2 tablespoons of water, and cornstarch together. Set this aside for later. Next, add the whipping cream and 1 cup of water and let it simmer for 2 minutes. Gradually whisk the grated cheese into the pan. Save one handful of the cheese for later. Once the cheese is added, slowly and gradually whisk in the egg and cornstarch mixture. Lower the heat and barely simmer for 3 to 4 minutes, stirring the entire time with a wooden spoon. It is very easy and likely that this sauce will scorch on the bottom, but stirring is a great way to prevent this. Remove this from the heat and add the cayenne, salt, lemon juice, lemon zest, and tarragon. Preheat your oven to 350°F. Add the cooked pasta to the cheese sauce and stir it very well. Next, stir in the lobster meat. Transfer this mixture to individual dishes or to an 8-inch baking pan. Sprinkle the remaining cheese on top, and generously coat with bread crumbs. Place in the oven. Bake for 20 minutes if in a larger pan, or bake for 8 minutes if prepared individually.

plating

If done individually, warn people how hot this is. If done in a large format, stick a serving spoon in it and place a big bowl next to that.

rock shrimp po' boy

with lettuce, tomato, and creole remoulade

serves 4

creole remoulade

2 egg yolks

2 fluid ounces champagne vinegar

1 Tablespoon creole mustard

2 teaspoons prepared creole
  seasoning

1 Tablespoon capers, rinsed

1 Tablespoon cornichons or gherkins,
  roughly chopped

½ cup grapeseed oil

Salt and pepper, as desired

rock shrimp po' boy with lettuce and tomato

3 fluid ounces cooking oil

½ pound fresh rock shrimp

4 light and fluffy hoagie (sub) rolls,
  split

8 leaves iceberg lettuce

2 roma tomatoes, sliced in ¼-inch
  slices

what to drink

- Pinot Blanc
- Lager beer
- French 75

what to ask the fish guy

Just ask how old they are. They are normally out of the shell and clean. If they are more than 5 days from the date that they were caught, reconsider buying.

method: creole remoulade

In a food processor or a blender, add the egg yolks and vinegar. Mix on a medium speed for 1 minute. Next, add the creole mustard and creole seasoning and mix for 1 more minute. Add the capers and little pickles and mix for another 30 seconds. Drizzle in the oil while still mixing on medium speed. Adjust the seasoning with salt and pepper as desired.

method: rock shrimp po' boy with lettuce and tomato

Set a large frying pan on the stove over a high heat, and coat the bottom of the pan with the cooking oil. Place the shrimp in the pan. Move them around until they have cooked through, approximately 2 to 3 minutes, and take them out of the pan. Next, spread the remoulade on the inside of the rolls. Place the lettuce leaves and tomato slices on top, and fill the rolls with the cooked rock shrimp.

plating

This is quite straight forward; just serve them as is.

sautéed fluke

with grilled scallions, poached egg, and caviar cream

---

serves 4

1 cup sour cream

Salt and pepper, as desired

1 ounce Hackleback caviar or
   domestic wild caviar

1 cup white wine vinegar

1 bunch scallions, stems removed

1 fluid ounce cooking oil

4 (5-ounce) fluke filets, skin off

4 eggs

---

what to drink

- Brut champagne
- Chardonnay
- Märzen
- Vodka martini

what to ask the fish guy

Ask for the fluke to be cut into 5 ounce portions and to be skin off. If they don't have fluke, halibut and petrale sole are great substitutions.

method

Whisk the sour cream and season with a pinch of salt and pepper. Fold in half of the caviar and refrigerate both for later. Set a pot of water to boil. Add the vinegar. When it boils, lower it to a simmer and let it sit for a few more minutes. Fire up the grill; scrape it, brush it, and oil it very well. Toss the scallions in 1 fluid ounce of cooking oil and a pinch of salt, and grill them for 3 to 4 minutes or until soft. Reserve them for later.

Set a frying pan on the stove over a medium-high heat, and add enough cooking oil to coat the bottom of the pan. Season the fluke portions lightly with salt and pepper. Pat them dry with a towel. When the oil begins to smoke, place the fish in the pan and cook for 30 seconds. Turn the heat down to medium, and using a spatula, move the fish a bit to make sure they don't stick. Cook for 2 minutes and flip them over. Cook for another two minutes and they will be ready. While the fish is cooking, exactly when you flip them over, crack open the eggs and gently place them in the simmering water and vinegar pot. To poach the eggs, gently swirl the water so that the they move in a circular fashion. This helps the white form around the yolk so that they cook more evenly. Using a slotted spoon, remove the eggs after 3 minutes.

plating

Begin by placing the scallions down on the plate first. Then, place the fish over the scallions, and spoon some of the caviar cream next to it. Place the poached egg on the plate next, top each egg off with the remaining caviar, and you're ready to serve.

grilled halibut

with curried apples, pineapple, mint, sunflower seeds, and avocado

serves 4

1 Tablespoon curry powder

1 cup Fuji apple, peeled, small diced

Salt and pepper, as desired

1 cup pineapple, peeled, small diced

½ cup salted, roasted sunflower
    seeds

1 ripe avocado, peeled, diced

2 Tablespoons extra-virgin olive oil

Zest of 1 lime

Juice of 1 lime

2 fluid ounces cooking oil

4 (5-ounce) halibut filets, skin off

what to drink

- Alvarinho
- Viognier
- Hefeweizen
- Piña colada

what to ask the fish guy

Ask for Alaskan halibut. It is the most sustainable and yields the highest amount. Have her or him cut you 5 ounce portions, and ask for the skin to be removed.

method

Fire up the grill. In case you've forgotten, scrape, brush, and generously oil it. In a small mixing bowl, mix the curry powder, diced apples, and a pinch of salt. In a separate bowl, mix everything else except the halibut, and adjust seasoning with salt and pepper. Rub the cooking oil over the portions of halibut generously, and lightly season them with salt and pepper. Place the halibut filets on the hot grill, and move them around every 30 seconds to cook evenly. Cook for 3 minutes and flip over. Repeat the previous step, and cook for another 3 minutes, or until the halibut has just cooked through. The meat will look cooked but still be glistening with moisture. Remove from the grill. Let's get to plating.

plating

Set the pineapple and sunflower seed mixture on the plate, and add some of the curried apples to this garnish. Set the cooked fish on top, and drizzle some of the liquid from the pineapple mixture on and around the fish. Serve and enjoy!

grilled day-boat scallops

with roasted cauliflower, shishito peppers, and heirloom tomato salsa

serves 4

heirloom tomato salsa

2 cups of heirloom tomatoes, washed, stems removed, and roughly chopped

1 cup of cucumber, peeled, seeds removed, roughly chopped

½ red onion, peeled and roughly chopped

2 Tablespoons of extra-virgin olive oil

1 Tablespoon of sherry vinegar

1 Tablespoon of cilantro leaves, destemmed, roughly chopped

Salt and pepper, as desired

grilled day-boat scallops

1 fluid ounce cooking oil

2 cups of cauliflower florets, cut from the stem

2 cups shishito peppers

12 U-10 day-boat scallops, cleaned

what to drink

- Sauvignon blanc
- Rosé from Provence
- Mexican lager
- Margarita on the rocks, no salt

what to ask the fish guy

First, ask if they will clean them for you—in the US, scallops usually make it to market already cleaned, as many parts outside the obvious meat are not the most beautiful; many are quite delicious though, such as the roe. Next, ask if the scallops are previously frozen. It's not the end of the world if they are, but it makes cooking them a bit more challenging. You want fresh day-boat scallops. If they are from the northeast Atlantic seaboard, you found the best.

method: heirloom tomato salsa

In a food processor or blender, place the chopped tomatoes, cucumber, red onion, olive oil, sherry vinegar, cilantro, and a pinch of salt and pepper. Blend quickly, pulsing so that the salsa remains a bit chunky. Adjust seasoning with salt and pepper and reserve for later.

method: grilled day-boat scallops

Set a large frying pan over medium-high heat. Add enough cooking oil to coat the bottom of the pan, and when it smokes, add the cauliflower florets. Turn the heat down to low-medium. Regularly stir, and cook them for 7 to 8 minutes or until they start to become tender. Then, add the peppers. Cook for 3 to 4 more minutes and season with salt and pepper. Reserve for later.

Turn on the grill and get it hot. Scrape it clean, brush it even cleaner, and oil it generously. Lightly rub oil on the scallops and season lightly with salt and pepper. Place them on the hot grill and move them every few seconds. Cook on the same side for 1½ minutes and flip them over. While still moving them around the grill, cook for another 1½ minutes and remove from the grill. They will still feel a bit raw, which is what you want. If you want to cook them more, you can, but don't blame me for the dry and stringy end result.

plating

Spoon a generous amount of salsa onto the plate. Add the cauliflower and peppers, and place 3 scallops on top. Serve immediately.

pan-roasted rock cod

with blood orange, baby beets, brussels sprouts, and horseradish vinaigrette

serves 4

warm horseradish vinaigrette

1 cup grapeseed oil

½ cup red wine vinegar

2 Tablespoons fresh horseradish, grated

1 whole shallot, peeled, minced

Salt and pepper, as desired

pan-roasted cod

2 bunches baby beets (chioggas are amazing if you can find them)

Salt and pepper, as desired

½ pound Brussels sprouts, cut lengthwise into ¼-inch pieces

4 (5-ounce) rock cod filets, skin on

3 fluid ounces cooking oil

1 Tablespoon whole oregano leaves, destemmed

2 blood oranges, skin removed, cut into segments

what to drink

- Rosé champagne
- Beaujolais
- Rauchbier
- Sidecar

what to ask the fish guy

Ask for the thicker side of the cod loin, and let them know you want the portions to be 5 ounces each. Although it might sound like you are asking a lot, ask them to leave the skin on and slightly score the skin down the middle. This shouldn't be a problem as they have the knives and they are cutting this for you anyway. By scoring the skin, the fish will cook more evenly as the skin will stay in the cooking oil throughout the process. If not, there is a good possibility that the fish will buckle or curve away from the oil, leaving the center uncooked.

method: warm horseradish vinaigrette

In a blender, combine the grapeseed oil, vinegar, horseradish, minced shallot, and a pinch of salt and pepper. Mix for 30 seconds and transfer to a small sauce pot. Place over low heat.

method: pan roasted cod

Preheat your oven to 350°F. Wash the beets with cold water. Toss them in salt, enough to coat the outside of each, and place them on a baking tray. Roast them in the oven for 20 to 25 minutes or until they are soft and cooked through. Let them cool. Once cool, use a paring knife to scrape the skins away. If you have latex gloves, you should wear them. Otherwise, the beets will leave your hands a lovely shade of red. Cut the beets into quarters and set aside for later. Next, bring a pot of lightly salted water to a boil, and add the Brussels sprouts. Cook for 2 minutes, strain them from the boiling water, and quickly rinse with cold running water. Set them aside for later.

Set a frying pan for the fish on a separate burner. Season the fish lightly with salt and pepper, and pat the skin side dry with a paper towel. Coat the bottom of this frying pan with 1 fluid ounce of cooking oil, bring it to a smoking point, and place the fish in the oil with the skin side down. Lower the heat to medium. After 30 seconds, move the fish around with a spatula to make sure the skin isn't sticking to the pan, and press on the filet all over to force the skin to cook in the oil. Normally, it will resist, as it has such a high water content, but a few little encouraging pushes will make the skin cook beautifully. Cook for 5 minutes and turn the filets over. Toss the Brussels sprouts with the remaining cooking oil, place on a baking tray with the peeled beets, and put them into the oven. Let them roast for 5 minutes. After 3 minutes, take

Continued on page 166

the fish out of the pan and set aside for plating. Then, remove the tray from the oven, sprinkle the oregano leaves throughout, and adjust seasoning with salt and pepper.

plating

Set a mix of Brussels sprouts and beets on the plate. Add the blood orange segments and set the cooked fish on top. Drizzle the warm horseradish vinaigrette around the plate and serve immediately.

grilled albacore

with pretzel spoon bread, roasted squash, and carrot ginger sauce

serves 4

carrot ginger sauce

1 large carrot, peeled, cut into pieces

1 whole shallot, peeled, sliced

1 Tablespoon fresh ginger, grated

½ cup white wine

½ cup heavy whipping cream

Juice of 1 lime

Salt and pepper, as desired

grilled albacore with pretzel spoon bread and roasted squash

6 eggs

3 cups whole milk

1 cup heavy whipping cream

Juice of 1 lemon

Zest of 1 lemon

2 Tablespoons prepared roasted garlic

1 Tablespoon tarragon leaves, destemmed, roughly chopped

1 pound fresh pretzels, cut into bite-sized cubes, toasted

1 Tablespoon unsalted butter, softened

1 butternut squash, peeled, stems removed, cut into pieces

Zest of 1 lime

4 (5-ounce) albacore loins

what to drink

- Gruener Vetliner
- Pinot Noir
- Belgian triple

what to ask the fish guy

Oddly enough, albacore is one of the few fishes that can handle being frozen. If it was previously frozen, ask if it was blast frozen at sea. This is the best way. If it's fresh, that's great too. Also, Oregon and California are fishing some great albacore, so always go the domestic route. It's tough to argue that fresh and local are always the best choice.

method: carrot ginger sauce

In a sauce pot, cook the carrot over medium heat for 3 to 4 minutes, then add the shallot and ginger. Lower the heat and cook for 3 more minutes. Add the wine, and cook for 2 minutes or until it's almost dry. Add the cream, lime juice, and a pinch of salt and pepper. Cook for 5 more minutes or until the carrots are tender. Transfer this to a blender and purée. (Remember, hot stuff in a blender means that we need to have a towel covering the lid and a hand firmly on that towel). Purée until smooth, adjusting the salt, pepper, and lime. If it's too thick, a splash of water will help to thin it out. Reserve for later.

method: grilled albacore with pretzel spoon bread and roasted squash

Preheat oven to 325°F. In a mixing bowl, whisk together the eggs, milk, cream, lemon juice, lemon zest, roasted garlic, and tarragon. Once it is mixed completely, fold in the toasted pretzel pieces. Let this soak for 10 minutes. Using whole butter, generously grease a 9 x 9 x 2-inch baking pan or small loaf pan with butter. Using a large spoon, spoon the mixture into the pan, and pour any excess liquid from the bowl into the pan. Place the pan in the preheated oven. This will take between 45 minutes to 1 hour. You will know when it is ready as it will be spongy and no longer liquid. Set a timer for 30 minutes, and cover the bread pudding with foil once the 30 minutes have passed; this will prevent it from getting too dark. Now, set the timer for 15 minutes. If it isn't ready after that, check it every few minutes. Once it has set and feels like a spongy cake, remove it from the oven, remove the foil, and let it cool in the pan.

167

Continued on page 168

In a medium-sized frying pan, set over a medium heat and pan-roast the squash for 8 to 10 minutes, moving everything regularly. Once the pieces are fork tender, season with the salt, pepper, and lime zest. Set this aside for later.

Fire up the grill. Scrape it, brush it, and oil it very well. Drizzle some oil over the albacore and season it lightly with salt and pepper. Grill on each side for 2 to 3 minutes and remove from the grill. We want to cook it to medium.

plating

Scoop out a chunk of the spoon bread and set on the plate. Place some of the squash next to it, and drizzle the sauce all around the plate. Slice the albacore and set it on top. You're there.

smoked sockeye salmon

with quick spice bread, cardamom cream, and garlic cucumbers

serves 4

- 2 Tablespoons unsalted butter, softened + extra to grease the cake pan
- 2 cups all-purpose flour
- 1½ teaspoons baking soda
- 1 teaspoon ground cinnamon
- 1 teaspoon powdered ginger
- ½ teaspoon allspice
- ½ teaspoon ground nutmeg
- Zest of 1 lime
- 1 egg
- ½ cup molasses
- 1 cup water
- 1 cup sour cream
- Juice of 1 lime
- 1 Tablespoon ground cardamom
- Salt and pepper, as desired
- 1 cup cucumbers, peeled, thinly sliced
- 1 Tablespoon prepared garlic
- 1 Tablespoon extra-virgin olive oil
- 1 Tablespoon champagne vinegar
- 1 Tablespoon fresh dill, destemmed, chopped
- 12 ounces smoked sockeye salmon

what to drink

- Aquavit
- Vouvray
- Brown ale
- Old-fashioned

what to ask the fish guy

You might be on your own here. Typically, you will find this in a case next to the smoked fish and pre-packaged products. If you cannot find it there, ask if they have any behind their counter, and ask where it's from. If you can't find sockeye, try to stay with pacific wild king salmon.

method

Preheat your oven to 350°F, and grease a small cake or loaf pan with butter. Then, flour it, shaking out any excess flour. In a mixing bowl, combine the flour, baking soda, cinnamon, ginger, allspice, nutmeg, and lime zest. In a separate bowl, preferably an electric mixer, combine the egg, butter, molasses, and water. Combine the two bowls together and pour the batter into the buttered and floured cake pan. Bake for 30 to 40 minutes or until cooked through. Using a fork, stick it in the cake, and if it comes out clean, you're all set. Let it cool for 15 minutes before removing from the pan.

Whisk the sour cream in a mixing bowl. Add the lime juice and ground cardamom. Adjust seasoning with salt and pepper and reserve for later. Marinate the sliced cucumbers with the garlic, olive oil, vinegar, and dill.

plating

Slice the spice bread and quickly toast the slices in the oven. Arrange the cream, salmon, and cucumbers on a plate. Serve the bread on the side. Essentially, the idea is to allow people to spoon the cream, top with the cucumbers and salmon, and make the proportions how they would like.

seared yellowfin tuna

with toasted pumpkin seeds, chestnut butter, pear, fennel, and grapefruit

---

serves 4

2 fluid ounces cooking oil

1 bulb fennel, cut into 8 wedges

4 (4–5-ounce) yellowfin ahi tuna
  portions

½ cup chestnut butter, softened

2 cups wild arugula

½ cup roasted, salted pumpkin seeds

2 ripe pears, peeled, stem and seeds
  removed, diced

1 grapefruit, skin and pith removed,
  cut into segments

Salt and pepper, as desired

what to drink

- Chardonnay
- Hard cider
- Calvados

what to ask the fish guy

Ask if they have #1 or #1+ grade tuna. #2+ is fine but usually has more waste. Next, make sure it is handline caught. Hawaiian longline and free school are reasonable second choices, but avoid the troll-caught stuff. Ask them to remove the skin and bloodline for you and to cut 4 (4–5-ounce) portions, preferably from the center of the loin. If they can cut you small blocks versus thin steaks, you will be much happier.

method

Set two frying pans on the stove, and add 1 fluid ounce of cooking oil to each. Turn the heat to high, and in one pan, add the fennel. Cook for 2 minutes then lower the heat to medium, constantly moving the fennel around so that it cooks evenly. Cook for 10 to 12 minutes. Season the tuna portions with salt and pepper. Place the tuna in the other pan, leaving it on high, and cook to just color the outside while keeping the fish very rare. Remove the tuna from the pan, and check on the fennel. Once it is soft, it's time to plate.

plating

Smear some chestnut butter on the plate, and arrange the wild arugula, pumpkin seeds, pears, grapefruit, and cooked fennel on the plate. Slice the tuna, and arrange it as desired over this garnish. If you like, a little sprinkle of salt on the sliced tuna is a great way to go.

tuna sashimi

with grilled apple salsa, mint leaves, toasted sesame, and mustard seed oil

---

serves 4

2 green apples, peeled, cores
    removed, diced

1 Tablespoon red onions, minced

Juice of 1 lime

Zest of 1 lime

1 teaspoon sesame oil

Salt and pepper, as desired

12 ounces sashimi or sushi grade
    yellowfin tuna

½ cup mint leaves, destemmed

1 Tablespoon mustard seed oil

1 Tablespoon toasted sesame seeds

---

what to drink

- Gewürztraminer
- Bandol rosé
- Kölsch
- Pisco sour

what to ask the fish guy

Ask if they have #1 or #1+ grade tuna. #2+ is fine but usually has more waste. Make sure it is handline caught. Hawaiian longline and free school are reasonable second choices, but avoid the troll-caught stuff. Ask them to remove the skin and bloodline for you, as well. This will leave you with a ready-to-dice product. If they are not too busy and you seem to be getting along, you could even ask that they thinly slice it sashimi style. I bet a gift of beautiful beer might make this deal more attractive to our friend behind the counter . . . just sayin'.

method

Fire up that grill; scrape it, brush it, and oil it generously. In a mixing bowl, combine the diced apple, red onions, lime juice, lime zest, sesame oil, and a pinch of salt and pepper. Set this salsa aside for later. Slice the tuna as thinly as possible.

plating

Arrange the tuna slices on plates as you wish. This is a great appetizer, but it can also be served as a shared item, family style, or on a buffet. Place the apple salsa around the tuna. Scatter some mint leaves, drizzle a bit of mustard seed oil, and sprinkle the tuna with a touch of salt and sesame seeds. Serve as cold as possible.

sweet potato and ginger tarte

with cinnamon pear sauce and angel food cake croutons

serves 6

cinnamon pear sauce

1 teaspoon vanilla extract

Juice of 4 limes

Zest of 2 limes

2 Tablespoons ground cinnamon, plus extra for seasoning

2 ripe pears, peeled, destemmed, deseeded, roughly chopped

Sugar, for seasoning

sweet potato and ginger tarte with angel food cake croutons

2 slices prepared angel food cake

½ cup granulated sugar

½ cup unsalted butter, softened

3 eggs

½ cup heavy whipping cream

1 Tablespoon pickled ginger, roughly chopped

1 teaspoon vanilla extract

Zest of 2 limes

1 teaspoon cinnamon

2 cups cooked sweet potatoes, mashed

1 unbaked 9-inch pie crust

what to ask the fish guy

It's probably time to invite this person over for dinner after all they have done for you.

what to drink

- Moscato d'Asti
- Sauternes
- Pumpkin ale

method: cinnamon pear sauce

In a blender, purée the lime juice, lime zest, the 2 tablespoons of ground cinnamon, and the chopped pear. Adjust seasoning with cinnamon and sugar as desired and reserve for later.

method: sweet potato and ginger tart with angel food cake croutons

Preheat your oven to 375°F. Cut little cubes out of the angel food cake, and place on a baking tray. Place in the oven and let them cook for 5 minutes. Take them out once they have just begun to toast, and reserve for later. They should be barely turning golden brown.

Turn the oven temperature to 350°F. In an electric mixer, or by hand in a mixing bowl, mix the sugar and butter together first. Add the eggs one at a time. Next, add the cream, ginger, vanilla, lime zest, cinnamon, and cooked sweet potato mash. Mix it well, and spoon this filling into the unbaked pie crust. Bake for 30 to 40 minutes or until the filling is set and you can stick a fork in it and it comes out clean.

plating

Cut pie slices. Drizzle the sauce over it and then sprinkle some of the croutons on and around the slices. Serve warm or cold; it works both ways.

whole roasted fish taco bar

with guacamole, salsa, grated cheese, lime, and cilantro leaves

---

serves 8

4 avocados

1 red onion, peeled, small diced

6 limes, 4 cut into wedges, 2 juiced and zested (set aside for later)

1 cup cilantro leaves, ½ chopped, ½ left whole for presentation

Salt and pepper, as desired

5 ripe tomatoes, roughly chopped

3 Tablespoons extra-virgin olive oil

2 Tablespoons sherry vinegar

1 Teaspoon cayenne pepper

2 Tablespoons fresh oregano leaves, chopped

1 cucumber, peeled, seeds removed, diced

1 head Napa cabbage, finely shaved

1 big fish (see pg. 181 for suggestions)

2 cups grated organic Monterey jack cheese

1 cup organic sour cream

20 tortillas

---

what to drink with this recipe

- Have to leave this one a bit vague as so many people are at this party, but make sure you have a full bar, cold beer, and margaritas

method

Cut each avocado in half and remove the pit. Scoop out the avocado and chop it. In a mixing bowl, add the red onion, lime juice and zest, and the chopped cilantro leaves. Adjust seasoning with salt and pepper as desired and set aside.

Place the chopped tomatoes in a mixing bowl. Add the extra-virgin olive oil, sherry vinegar, cayenne pepper, chopped oregano, and diced cucumber. Season with salt and pepper as desired and set aside.

Toss the finely sliced cabbage in lime juice and season with a small pinch of salt. Set this aside. Have the grated cheese ready and on the table with the guacamole, salsa, sour cream, and tortillas. It is a nice touch to grill or toast tortillas prior to setting the buffet; they lend to a much nicer dining experience. Once the fish is cooked and the ingredients are ready, it's really about setting everything out and letting your guests have at it. Please note that everything should be on the table while the fish is cooking and almost ready; it tastes the very best when it comes directly out of the oven. If you decide to offer rice and beans, that should also be kept hot to ensure that none of it is served cold.

plating

Set all components in separate bowls for serving buffet style. Have all ingredients laid out on the table as the fish is just finishing. Set the fish on a cutting board, and have some kitchen towels available to soak up the mess. This is messy business but well worth it.

what to ask the fish guy

Regardless of the species of fish you have selected, you want the whole fish, gutted, gilled, and scaled. If they seem amenable to all of this, ask that they gently score the sides. Ask that they make a few slices vertically along the filet, and a few on both sides of the vertebrae. This makes it much easier to remove the cooked filet from the carcass after whole roasting.

the whole fish and larger gatherings

It is always a fun and rather spectacular moment at the restaurant when someone orders the whole fish. Depending on what is caught that day, we feature a wide variety of species and sizes. My favorite is when the wild king salmon season opens and we manage to get our hands on a fifteen to twenty-pounder. A closer runner up is the American day-boat snapper, rod-and-reel-caught out of the Gulf of Mexico. I prefer those around the six-pound size because, as they get bigger, the filets become less meat and more bones, yielding less fish, but you still have to pay for all of that waste. On the east coast, usually in summer, pulling in those eight- to ten-pound striped bass is pretty amazing too.

What these three fish all have in common is that you can serve eight to ten people with one whole fish, and you can do it in a number of ways. The first step is to have the fish guy remove the gills, remove the scales, and then remove the guts. Ask them to rinse it for you on the inside as well. Next, ask that they score (cut, but not too deep) along the dorsal and intermittently along the filets. The idea is to oven-roast this, and these little cuts will ultimately make removing pieces of the filets a lot easier. Now, flip back through the recipes and pick one that you want to multiply by two. Gather your ingredients, get the kitchen set, but the only difference

here is how we are going to prepare and serve the big fish.

One of the best ways to serve this, which keeps things very casual and easy, is to set the table for a "build-your-own-taco-bar." If you are restricted on time, going to the store and grabbing some grated cheese, tortillas, prepared guacamole, prepared salsa, limes, fresh cilantro, and some prepared rice and beans makes this incredibly easy and fun to serve.

For any of the fish mentioned above, preheat your oven to 500° F. Fill the cavity of the fish where the guts used to be with some chopped garlic, cut lemons, and fresh herbs. Also, crumple up enough parchment paper to completely fill them, and stand the fish up on an oiled parchment paper-lined baking tray. If you have silicon mats, they are the best and are quite bulletproof in the sense of avoiding sticking. Once the fish is standing, generously rub it with cooking oil, and generously sprinkle the outside with salt and pepper.

Whether you are going to set up an amazing and easy-to-produce taco bar, or if the plan is to pick a recipe from this book and multiply it, you have already made a remarkably good decision. Below is a quick table, indicating the aforementioned species, and it lists them by weight, the time it will take to cook them, and how many people they will feed. Please remember that the oven should be set to 500° F.

Whole Fish	6–8 pounds	8–10 pounds	10–12 pounds
Salmon	8 people 25 minutes	10 people 30 minutes	12 people 35 minutes
Red Snapper	6 people 30 minutes	8 people 35–40 minutes	8 people 45 minutes
Striped Bass	7–8 people 35 minutes	9–10 people 40 minutes	9–10 people 45 minutes

It's a good idea to have the dinner table set, cocktails or wine on the table, and everyone nearby when the fish has ten to twelve minutes remaining on the timer. Corralling people can be quite like herding cats, so having the table set and drinks ready while the fish is finishing up in the oven is a good idea. It is also an impressive sight as it leaves the oven and is presented to the group. I would serve it on the hot baking tray, placed on the stove where the guests can help themselves. It's tough to transfer them while they are cooked, as they will be delicate. Leaving it on the hot tray will also keep the fish warm. Have a serving fork and your metal spatula available for the folks to have at it! Most of the recipes in this book can be multiplied by two or three and their accompaniments work well for a buffet option. Substituting this whole fish preparation is always a lot of fun—so is cooking and eating fish!

I truly hope this book is useful for you and perhaps makes you consider better fish choices at home and dining out, gives you a better sense of confidence to replace meat every once in a while, and offers more opportunities for wonderful, memorable dining and gathering experiences to happen more regularly.

about the author

Matthew Dolan is an established chef and restaurant owner who trained at The Culinary Institute of America in New York. His restaurant, Twenty Five Lusk, was named *Esquire* magazine's Best New Restaurant and OpenTable Diners' Choice Top Hot Spot Restaurants in the United States since its opening in 2010. He resides in San Francisco, California.

acknowledgments

Anne-Claire Thieulon Dolan, thank you for making life make sense, your intense effort, and sheer existence

Sebastien and Luke Dolan, thank you for your patience and for being my amazing little dudes

Dad, Christine and Charlie, Will and Tory, and my brother Steve

Chad Bourdon, my friend and business partner of Twenty Five Lusk and Tap [415]

Elisa Celli, my agent and colleague from Bella Vita Literary

Twenty Five Lusk and its amazing team: Chef Kaili Hill, pastry chef extraordinaire Jean-Michel Boucard, Donnie Clark, Lauren Roberts, Cezar Kusik, and Josh Ansel

Fish Revolution's Crystal Sanders

Maggie Ostadahl from San Francisco's Aquarium of the Bay

Colin LaFrenze, the first guy to be my guide through all of this

TwoXSea's Kenny Belov, a role model and inspiration for all

Royal Hawaiian Seafood, Arfin "Feen" Thien, Leo Thien

BiRite Foodservice Distributors, Bill and Steve Barulich, and the man that makes it all happen, my friend and colleague Jim Latham

Hog Island Oyster Company, Marshall, California

Aloha Seafood, Mitch Gronner, and John

Nick's Cove, Marshall, California

Greenleaf Produce, Brisbane, California

Sebastopol Microgreens, Sebastopol, California

Drew Nieporent

Jennifer Waryas

Paula Daniels

My uncle Bob Dolan (just because I love the guy)

resources

Below is a handful of resources all provided by the believers—the spectacular people doing much more important work than I ever will!

Fish Revolution

Fish Revolution provides simple steps for consumers to navigate purchasing sustainable seafood either in restaurants or at the grocery store. Additionally, they work with businesses to implement sustainable seafood practices into their business policies to increase the amount of sustainable seafood available to consumers.

Seafood Watch

Seafood Watch, a program of Monterey Bay Aquarium, provides science-based recommendations that indicate which seafood items are "Best Choices" or "Good Alternatives," and which ones you should "Avoid." The Seafood Watch app is an excellent tool for consumers to use while shopping for seafood or dining in restaurants that guides them to a sustainable choice when asking the questions above.

Fish Watch

Fish Watch is positioned to help people make smart seafood choices by arming them with the facts about what makes US seafood sustainable—from the ocean or farm to your plate. Also, people will get up-to-date information on the status of some of the nation's most valuable marine fish harvested in US federal waters as well as US farmed fish that help meet our country's growing seafood demand. It is not a buyer's guide nor does it provide any certification or ecolabels.

Smithsonian National Museum of Natural History's Ocean Portal

The Washington D.C.-based Smithsonian Museum has created this resource to assist the user in learning more about sustainable consumer choices, cooking and recipes, and how to "look for the label"; one of the many available seafood labeling programs that can help you learn more about making the most sustainable seafood choice.

Marine Stewardship Council

The MSC is an international non-profit organization established to address the problem of unsustainable fishing and safeguard seafood supplies for the future. Using our fisheries certification and seafood labeling program, the MSC works with partners to promote sustainable fishing and transform markets. The MSC's certification and ecolabeling program enables everybody to play a part in securing a healthy future for our oceans.

Scripps Institute of Oceanography

A department of UC San Diego, Scripps Institution of Oceanography is one of the oldest, largest, and most important centers for ocean, earth, and atmospheric science research, education, and public service in the world. Research at Scripps encompasses physical, chemical, biological, geological, and geophysical studies of the oceans, Earth, and planets. Scripps undergraduate and graduate programs provide transformative educational and research opportunities in ocean, earth, and atmospheric sciences, as well as degrees in climate science and policy and marine biodiversity and conservation.

glossary of terms

Ahi

Hawaiian name for both yellowfin and bigeye tuna.

Anadromous

Any fish migrating from the sea into freshwater rivers and lakes to spawn (i.e., salmon, striped bass, shad, and alewife). Fish that migrate in the reverse direction, from freshwater to the sea, are called catadromous.

Aquaculture

The farming of aquatic species in salt, brackish, or freshwater. About half of the seafood produced globally is from aquaculture operators.

Belly Burn

Condition where the bones of the belly wall separate from the flesh; a sign of poor handling. Left too long before gutting, digestive enzymes break down flesh adjacent to the intestines.

Benthos

The community of marine life inhabiting the sea floor.

Billfish

Pelagic fish whose upper jaws are prolonged into a spear or sword (e.g., swordfish).

Biomass

This is the total weight of a number of organisms or population of a species.

Bleeding

Process in which fish are bled while alive by severing an artery. The highest quality fish are bled.

Block

Seafood that has been frozen in a plate freezer under hydraulic pressure. Filet blocks, which are normally 16.5 pounds, are sawed into pieces and used to make a variety of breaded and battered products such as fish sticks. Raw, shell-on shrimp are often frozen in 2-kilo or 5-pound blocks, as is crabmeat.

Boneless

A filet that has all the bones removed.

Brine Freezing

Practice of freezing seafood by immersion in liquid brine, usually at temperatures of about 5°F. King, snow, and Dungeness crab are usually brine frozen.

Bullet

A term used to describe a finfish that has had its head, guts, and tail removed. Most often used with mahimahi or farmed sturgeon.

Burned (Or "Burnt")

A metabolic change to the flesh of a fish, most associated with tuna. When tuna are caught by troll or handline, they can struggle during capture. Since tuna are warm-blooded, they can literally cook or burn their flesh due to metabolic changes. Burned tuna will have a lighter color, softer texture, and a reduced shelf life.

Bushel

A unit of measure equal to 32 quarts or 8 gallons. Most often used when selling live mollusks like clams, oysters, and mussels.

Bycatch

Fish and other marine life that are incidentally caught while fishing for the target species. Bycatch is generally discarded dead while at sea and can include sea birds, turtles, marine mammals, juveniles of the target species, or targeted fish from other fisheries. Reduction of bycatch is an ongoing effort in many fisheries and is common criteria in wild seafood sustainability ratings and in assessing the overall sustainability evolution.

C&F

A shipping term which means the cost of freight is included in the quoted price; often called a "delivered" price.

Cast net

Nets usually cast from shore or a boat that catches fish by falling on top of them and then closing, typically restricted to shallow waters.

Catadromous

Species spawn at sea and then their young migrate to fresh or brackish water to grow and mature (e.g., American eel); opposite of anadromous.

Catch

The total number of fish and marine life taken by fishers from an area over a given period of time, including bycatch.

Caviar

Legally in the US, only salted sturgeon eggs can be labeled simply caviar. Eggs or roe from other species must be labeled to include the species of fish (i.e., salmon caviar, paddlefish roe, etc).

Cello Pack

Packages or block-shaped wraps of frozen filets (traditionally from North Atlantic groundfish species like cod and haddock) wrapped in plastic cellophane or polyethylene film, typically packed six packages to a 5-pound box. Each package is graded by the number of filets per wrap (i.e., 1/3 cellos contain 1 to 3 filets per wrap).

Ciguatera

A type of potentially fatal poisoning associated with reef fish that ingest the ciguatoxin. It is not a result of poor handling.

CO-Treated

Fish filets that have been exposed to carbon monoxide, which is used to retain or enhance red color.

Copepods

A large group of small crustaceans and an important food source for larger species such as fish, seabirds, and baleen whales.

Crayfish

In the US, the name associated with small, lobster-like crustaceans, which are also known as crawfish. Overseas, the name is sometimes used to describe spiny, or rock lobsters.

Crustacean

Invertebrates characterized by a segmented body (with limbs that are paired and jointed) and exoskeleton (e.g., lobsters, crabs, and shrimp).

Cryogenic

Extremely cold freezing process, usually using liquid nitrogen or carbon dioxide. Because of its higher cost, most often used to freeze costlier species such as shrimp and lobster.

Demersal

Refers to fish living close to the bottom of a body of water, such as cod or flounder. Synonymous with groundfish or bottomfish.

Dragger

A term for a trawler, a boat that tows a large net behind it.

Dredge

A heavy mesh gear that sucks up everything from the seafloor, used primarily to target shellfish. The impacts of dredge gear on benthos habitats is an environmental concern.

Dressed

Fish that has been gutted and had the entrails removed.

Drift Net

A large gillnet suspended vertically by floats that drifts in the open ocean. Drift nets are banned in international waters due to their indiscriminate catch and are limited to 1.5 miles in length in US waters.

Dry

A reference to a product that has not had water added it to by using STP.

Essential Fish Habitat

The water and substrate necessary for fish to reproduce, feed, and grow to maturity as defined by the US Congress in the 1996 Sustainable Fisheries Act.

Estuary

An ecosystem defined as the intersection of a freshwater river and a saltwater body (oceans) that serve as nurseries for juvenile fish and provide other ecosystem services.

Ex-Vessel Price

Price that a fisherman receives for his catch at the dock.

Exclusive Economic Zone (EEZ)

The typically 200-nautical mile zone from a country's coastal border that gives that country exclusive fishing rights as established by the international Law of the Sea.

Factory Boat

A large fishing boat that processes and freezes its catch on board in a processing factory. The level of processing may vary from simply heading and gutting fish to producing skinless, boneless filets.

FAS

Abbreviation for frozen-at-sea.

Farmed Seafood

Raising fish commercially in tanks or enclosures, usually for food. It is the principal form of aquaculture. A facility that releases juvenile fish into the wild for recreational fishing or to supplement a species' natural numbers is generally referred to as a fish hatchery.

Feed Conversion Ratio (FCR)

In aquaculture, this term is generally the ratio of how much food is used to produce the fish species, or more specifically the ratio of the amount of feed necessary to the gain in wet body weight of fish produced. The lower the ratio the better the situation, as wild seafood protein is often fed to grow farmed fish, resulting in a net loss of fish.

Filet

A strip of flesh from the side of a fish, cut away from the backbone. Filets can be skin-on or skinless, bone-in or boneless. If the bones are removed by cutting out a strip of flesh, the filet is v-cut. If the nape and bones are removed, it is a j-cut.

Filter Feeding Shellfish

All species of shell that feed by filtering microscopic particles from the water. This removes problematic sediments and phytoplankton and their associated nutrients. Oysters, clams, and abalone are good examples.

Finning

The process of removing sharks' fins and discarding the rest of the body, primarily used for soups in Asian markets; a practice banned in the United States in 2000.

Fishmeal

Fish or shellfish that are manipulated by drying, cooking, pressing, and/or grinding fish or shellfish as a protein source; used primarily in aquaculture operations for carnivorous fish.

Fishery Management Council

Eight regional councils in the US responsible for developing Fishery Management Plans (FMPs) for fisheries that exist in federal waters.

FOB

Free on board; a location usually follows, indicating the point at which any additional shipping charges are the buyer's responsibility.

Forage Fish

These small fishes form schools and are the primary food source for predator fish and seabirds. They typically feed on plankton, and their numbers can add up into the hundreds of thousands per school. Herring and mullet are two common examples.

Free School

Collective behavior by groups of fish. Any group of fish that stays together for social reasons is said to be shoaling; if the shoal is swimming in the same direction together, it is schooling. About one quarter of fish shoal all their lives, and about one half of fish shoal for part of their lives.

Freezer Burn

Dry, white crumbly spots on frozen seafood caused by dehydration. A sign that either the fish has been in the freezer a long time, or was not properly protected prior to freezing.

G&G

Head-on finfish that has been gilled and gutted. Typically done with higher-value species like red snapper, grouper, and king salmon.

Gaping

Separation of fish flesh, usually a sign of soft flesh and an indicator of poor handling.

Gillnet

A net designed to capture a fish by its gills. Many states have banned their use in coastal waters due to bycatch, but regulations on mesh size, net location, and timing of when nets are in the water have become increasingly common to reduce bycatch.

Grading

Size measurements by which seafood is often sold. Increments are most often either counts per pound (i.e., 21/25 shrimp) or by graded weights (i.e., 4–6 lb. H&G salmon or 2/4 oz. pollock filets).

Green

Term used to describe raw, frozen shellfish (i.e., green, headless shrimp); can also be used to describe the weight of seafood before it is processed (i.e., green weight).

Groundfish

A generic term to describe the different types of finfish that live on or near the seafloor such as cod, flounder, and rockfish.

H&G

Term used to describe fish that have had their heads and guts removed.

Handline

A fishing line principally managed by hand as opposed to the use of a rod to manage the line.

High-Grading

The fishing practice of retaining the most valuable target species being harvested and discarding the lesser valuable target species, often due to species characteristics such as size and color.

High Seas

The designation given to the ocean area that is not governed by any single country and where most fishing takes place.

Histamines

Chemicals produced by decomposition of flesh in scombroid species (i.e., tuna, mahi, mackerels) when fish are not adequately refrigerated. Rarely fatal, but can cause severe illness.

Hook-and-Line

A fishing method that uses natural or artificial bait placed on a hook fixed to the end of a line in both single and multiple units; often confused with longlines.

IQF

Individually Quick Frozen. Seafood that is IQF is normally protected with a glaze to prevent dehydration.

ITQ/IVQ

Individual Transferable Quota/Individual Vessel Quota. These are quotas that give fishermen ownership to harvest a specified amount of fish or shellfish. In most cases, they can be bought, sold, or leased.

IUU Fishing

Illegal, Unreported, Unregulated as it pertains to fishing that is conducted accordingly. Often referred to as pirate fishing, IUU fishing is a major threat to the sustainability of seafood, as there is very little way to account for how much seafood is being taken from the overall system. IUU undermines the integrity of management and legitimate fishers to harvest seafood responsibly.

Jig

A method of fishing that uses actively fished vertical lines onto which baited hooks are attached. (Also a dance that my ancestry created thanks to a lack of rhythm and whiskey.)

Landings

The quantity of fish/shellfish brought ashore for sale, not including possible bycatch caught and discarded at sea.

Loin

The thickest part of a filet, above the belly cavity. Can also be used to describe boneless quarters from large fish like tuna and swordfish.

Longline

A fishing method that uses several short lines with baited hooks attached to a main line that is dragged through the water. Longlines can contain thousands of hooks and extend for several miles and often result in high-levels of bycatch depending on the number of hooks, when the lines are in the water, and where they are being fished.

Maximum Sustainable Yield (MSY)

The maximum amount of a species that can be removed from its environment without diminishing the long-term health of the overall population; a term that is often used by scientists and fishery managers when making recommendations or establishing fishing limits.

Overcapitalization

The scenario where there are more fishermen and vessels in a fishery than is necessary to catch the available volume of target species; often leads to overfishing.

Overfishing

The scenario in which the amount of fish taken in a fishery is greater than the amount of the remaining fish population; a net loss in fish.

Pelagic

Fish that live off the bottom, often near the surface. Many pelagic species such as mahimahi, tuna, and swordfish are also highly migratory.

Pin bones

Fine bones which are often found along the midline of a filet. Most often used when describing salmon or trout bones.

Plankton

Small plant (phytoplankton) and animal (zooplankton) species that spend some or all of their life on the sea surface. Many marine species are planktonic in their life stages (e.g., cod, Dungeness crab) and they are the basis of the marine food web, providing food for such species as whale sharks and blue whales.

Pole

A fishing method where fish are attracted to bait placed in the water and then hooked with a line on the end of a pole and "poled" out of the water; used to capture surface-swimming fish such as yellowfin and skipjack tuna.

Pond

An aquaculture facility, either natural or man-made, with differing impacts on the environment based on how the discharge from the pond is handled. Many catfish, carp, and tilapia are produced in ponds.

Pot

A.k.a. "trap," a cage or basket usually placed on the seafloor connected by ropes to floating buoys on the sea surface.

Purse Seine

A net that encompasses a school of fish and then is drawn closed at the bottom like a purse.

Raceway

This term describes both the larger type of aquaculture system in which water is diverted from nearby streams or pumped from wells into concrete troughs where fish are held, and the troughs themselves, known as raceways.

Roe

Eggs from a fish or shellfish.

Sashimi

Thinly sliced pieces of fish or shellfish that are eaten raw. Also used (both accurately and inaccurately) to indicate a fish of premium or sashimi quality.

Section

A cooked crab portion that contains one half of a cleaned crab, including legs, claw, and shoulder.

Shatter pack

A carton of frozen filets similar to a layer pack, but layers are separated by a continuous interleaved polyethylene sheet. Individual filets can be separated by dropping or "shattering" the carton.

Stock

A distinct sub-population of a larger group of species that is reproductively isolated to some extent from other populations; in fishery management, the term can be used to describe one or more sub-populations of one or more species.

STP

Acronym for sodium triphosphate, a widely-used food additive. Although it is designed to prevent drip loss, in practice STP is used by processors to increase yields by adding water to a seafood product. In some cases, such as scallops, STP can allow a processor to gain 10 to 15 percent additional weight.

Steak

In smaller fish, such as salmon and halibut, the steak is a cross section of a fish, containing the backbone. In larger fish, such as tuna and swordfish, steaks are boneless portions cut from a loin.

Surimi

Raw extruded flesh from lower-value finfish like pollock and hake that is frozen in blocks and later used to make seafood alternatives.

Tail

The thin, tapered portion of a filet that normally does not contain bones.

Ton

A common unit of measurement. A metric ton contains 2,205 pounds, while a short ton contains 2,000 pounds.

Total Allowable Catch (TAC)

A fishery management term that defines the total amount of a target species that can be taken in a given time period, usually based on a fishing season or annual basis.

Tote

A large container used to hold fish or shellfish. Fresh seafood is iced and held in plastic totes until processing. Fiber totes are used to ship loose frozen H&G fish such as salmon and halibut to avoid the added cost of boxing fish.

Trap

A fishing method that uses a device, usually a cage or pot, that catch fish/shellfish within the device; typically baited with the cage designed for a specific species and often very little bycatch.

Trawl

A fishing method using a net with a wide mouth that tapers to a small end towed behind a fishing vessel at various depths of the sea including the bottom and mid-water levels. There are both habitat impact and bycatch concerns with trawl fishing because of the indiscriminate nature of the gear.

Troll Caught

A type of hook-and-line fishing method where one line or multiple unconnected lines, each with baited hooks, are towed behind a fishing vessel.

V-Cut

A cut that removes pin bones by making a v-shaped incision along both sides of the bone strip, leaving most of the nape.

index

A

aioli
    Salt Cod Croquettes, 79–80
albacore
    Grilled Albacore, 167–168
    Poached Albacore Salad, 95
allspice
    Smoked Sockeye Salmon, 171
    Upside Down Pineapple Cake, 47
almond milk
    Salt Cod Croquettes, 79–80
Almond Milk–Poached Rock Cod, 77
anchovy
    Pan-Fried Petrale Sole, 73
    Poached Albacore Salad, 95
angel food cake
    Sweet Potato and Ginger Tarte, 176
apples
    Beer-Steamed Mussels, 148
    Champagne-Poached Sole, 26
    Grilled Halibut, 160
    Seared Day-Boat Scallops, 8
    Steamed Manila Clams, 144
    Tuna Sashimi, 175
arctic char
    Crispy Arctic Char, 13–14
artichokes
    Chilled Lobster and Udon Noodle, 69
    Roasted Haddock Filet, 61–62
    Whole Roasted Dungeness Crab, 151

arugula
    Cod Melt, 127
    Grilled Halibut, 25
    Grilled Scallops, 107
    Lemon Sole Schnitzel, 29
    Sautéed Ling Cod, 33–34
    Seared Yellowfin Tuna, 172
    Smoked Trout Salad, 131
asparagus
    Chilled Poached Salmon, 85–86
    Garlic Prawns, 66
    Ginger and Asparagus Soup, 91
    Local Sand Dabs, 74
    Poached Lobster, 111
avocado
    Chilled Poached Salmon, 85–86
    Creole Gulf Prawns, 19–20
    Grilled Halibut, 160
    Grilled Scallops, 107
    Timeless Tuna Tartare, 135

B

bacon
    Baked Oysters, 53
    Roasted Haddock Filet, 61–62
    Soft-Shell Crab BLT, 65
    Whole Steamed Dungeness Crab, 16
Baked Local Sole, 123
Baked Oysters, 53
Barbecued Oysters, 143

basil
>   Almond Milk–Poached Rock
>   >   Cod, 77
>   Barbecued Oysters, 143
>   Crispy Arctic Char, 13–14
>   Garlic Prawns, 66
>   Grilled Halibut, 25
>   Grilled Prawn Salad, 112
>   Grilled Tuna Steak Frites, 87–88
>   Oysters on the Half Shell, 4
>   Pan-Fried Petrale Sole, 120
>   Pan-Seared Tru Cod, 124
>   Poached Lobster, 111
>   Poached Maine Lobster, 21–22
>   Shrimp and Coconut Soup, 116
>   Smoked Salmon and Farm Egg
>   >   Frittata, 38
>   Sweet Corn and Blueberry Pound
>   >   Cake, 136
>   Upside Down Pineapple Cake, 47
>   Yellowfin Tuna Ceviche, 41

bay leaf
>   Chilled Poached Salmon, 85–86
>   Grilled Halibut, 70

Bay Scallop Fish Tacos, 147

beans, kidney
>   Creole Gulf Prawns, 19–20

beer
>   Beer-Steamed Mussels, 148
>   Shandy-Steamed Steamer Clams, 104

Beer-Poached Mussels, 11–12

Beer-Steamed Mussels, 148

beets
>   Pan-Roasted Rock Cod, 165–166

bell pepper
>   Baked Local Sole, 123
>   Grilled Halibut, 119

blood orange
>   Pan-Roasted Rock Cod,
>   >   165–166

blueberries
>   Grilled Tuna Steak Frites, 87–88
>   Sweet Corn and Blueberry Pound
>   >   Cake, 136

Boquerónes
>   Pan-Fried Petrale Sole, 73

brandy
>   Pan-Roasted Prawns, 152

bread
>   Beer-Steamed Mussels, 148
>   Chilled Mussel Tea Sandwiches,
>   >   59–60
>   Cod Melt, 127
>   Pan-Fried Petrale Sole, 73
>   Rock Shrimp Po' Boy, 156
>   Rosé-Steamed Clams, 7
>   Sautéed Ling Cod, 33–34
>   Shandy-Steamed Steamer Clams, 104
>   Steamed Mussel Chowder, 108

bread crumbs
>   Dungeness Crab Rolls, 115
>   Lemon Sole Schnitzel, 29
>   Lobster Mac 'n Cheese, 155
>   Salmon Burgers, 132
>   Soft-Shell Crab BLT, 65

bread pudding
>   Sautéed Ling Cod, 33–34

Brie
>   Baked Oysters, 53

Brussels sprouts
>   Pan-Roasted Rock Cod, 165–166
>   Poached Maine Lobster, 21–22

butternut squash
>   Grilled Albacore, 167–168
>   Sautéed Ling Cod, 33–34

C

cabbage
>   Napa, 179
>   >   Grilled Prawn Salad, 112

savoy
 Bay Scallop Fish Tacos, 147
cake
 Sweet Corn and Blueberry Pound
  Cake, 136
 Sweet Potato and Ginger Tarte,
  176
 Upside Down Pineapple Cake, 47
calamari
 Skillet-Roasted Trout, 81–83
cantaloupe
 Pan-Seared Tru Cod, 124
capers
 Lemon Sole Schnitzel, 29
 Pan-Fried Petrale Sole, 120
 Rock Shrimp Po' Boy, 156
cardamom
 Rhubarb and Strawberry Crisp, 96
 Smoked Sockeye Salmon, 171
carrots
 Grilled Albacore, 167–168
 Poached Maine Lobster, 21–22
 Seared Yellowfin Tuna, 44
cauliflower
 Grilled Day-Boat Scallops, 163
 Seared Day-Boat Scallops, 8
caviar
 Sautéed Fluke, 159
cayenne
 Barbecued Oysters, 143
 Grilled Prawn Salad, 112
 Lobster Mac 'n Cheese, 155
 Whole Roasted Fish Taco Bar, 179
 Yellowfin Tuna Crudo, 92
celery
 Creole Gulf Prawns, 19–20
ceviche
 Day-Boat Scallop Ceviche, 56
 Oyster Ceviche, 103
 Yellowfin Tuna Ceviche, 41

champagne
 Champagne-Poached Sole, 26
Champagne-Poached Sole, 26
char
 Crispy Arctic Char, 13–14
cheese
 Brie
  Baked Oysters, 53
 cheddar
  Cod Melt, 127
  Lobster Mac 'n Cheese, 155
  Smoked Salmon and Farm Egg
   Frittata, 38
 Monterey Jack
  Whole Roasted Fish Taco Bar, 179
 Parmesan
  Pan-Roasted Tru Cod, 31–32
chervil
 Oyster Ceviche, 103
chestnut butter
 Seared Yellowfin Tuna, 172
chili flakes
 Seared Yellowfin Tuna, 44
Chilled Lobster and Udon Noodle, 69
Chilled Mussel Tea Sandwiches, 59–60
Chilled Poached Salmon, 85–86
chives
 Almond Milk–Poached Rock Cod, 77
 Baked Local Sole, 123
 Dungeness Crab Rolls, 115
 Poached Maine Lobster, 21–22
 Salt Cod Croquettes, 79–80
 Smoked Salmon and Farm Egg
  Frittata, 38
 Steamed Mussel Chowder, 108
cilantro
 Bay Scallop Fish Tacos, 147
 Day-Boat Scallop Ceviche, 56
 Creole Gulf Prawns, 19–20
 Grilled Day-Boat Scallops, 163

Grilled Prawn Salad, 112
Grilled Scallops, 107
Poached Lobster, 111
Timeless Tuna Tartare, 135
Whole Roasted Fish Taco Bar, 179
cinnamon
Rhubarb and Strawberry Crisp, 96
Sautéed Ling Cod, 33–34
Smoked Sockeye Salmon, 171
Sweet Potato and Ginger Tarte, 176
Upside Down Pineapple Cake, 47
clams
Clams on the Half Shell, 54
Rosé-Steamed Clams, 7
Shandy-Steamed Steamer Clams, 104
Steamed Manila Clams, 144
Clams on the Half Shell, 54
clementines
Local Sand Dabs, 74
coconut milk
Grilled Prawn Salad, 112
Shrimp and Coconut Soup, 116
cod
Almond Milk–Poached Rock
Cod, 77
Pan-Roasted Rock Cod, 165–166
Pan-Roasted Tru Cod, 31–32
Pan-Seared Tru Cod, 124
Salt Cod Croquettes, 79–80
Sautéed Ling Cod, 33–34
Cod Melt, 127
coriander
Grilled Halibut, 25, 70
Grilled Prawn Salad, 112
corn
Grilled Halibut, 119
Grilled Wild King Salmon, 128
Pan-Seared Tru Cod, 124
Poached Lobster, 111
Steamed Mussel Chowder, 108

Sweet Corn and Blueberry Pound
Cake, 136
cornichons
Rock Shrimp Po' Boy, 156
crab
Dungeness Crab Rolls, 115
Soft-Shell Crab BLT, 65
Whole Roasted Dungeness Crab, 151
Whole Steamed Dungeness Crab, 16
cream
Ginger and Asparagus Soup, 91
Grilled Albacore, 167–168
Grilled Halibut, 119
Lobster Mac 'n Cheese, 155
Pan-Roasted Prawns, 152
Rhubarb and Strawberry Crisp, 96
Salt Cod Croquettes, 79–80
Sautéed Ling Cod, 33–34
Sautéed Wild King Salmon, 43
Steamed Mussel Chowder, 108
Sweet Potato and Ginger Tarte, 176
crème fraîche
Bay Scallop Fish Tacos, 147
Creole Gulf Prawns, 19–20
creole seasoning
Creole Gulf Prawns, 19–20
Rock Shrimp Po' Boy, 156
Crispy Arctic Char, 13–14
croquettes
Salt Cod Croquettes, 79–80
cucumbers
Barbecued Oysters, 143
Day-Boat Scallop Ceviche, 56
Grilled Day-Boat Scallops, 163
Grilled Prawn Salad, 112
Grilled Wild King Salmon, 128
Oyster Ceviche, 103
Sautéed Wild King Salmon, 43
Smoked Sockeye Salmon, 171
Timeless Tuna Tartare, 135

Whole Roasted Fish Taco Bar, 179
curry powder
    Chilled Mussel Tea Sandwiches,
        59–60
    Grilled Halibut, 160

D
Day-Boat Scallop Ceviche, 56
dill
    Chilled Mussel Tea Sandwiches,
        59–60
    Smoked Sockeye Salmon, 171
    Steamed Mussel Chowder, 108
Dungeness Crab Rolls, 115

E
eggs
    Smoked Salmon and Farm Egg
        Frittata, 38
endives
    Sautéed Wild King Salmon, 43
escarole
    Crispy Arctic Char, 13–14
    Garlic Prawns, 66

F
fava leaves
    Poached Albacore Salad, 95
fennel
    Crispy Arctic Char, 13–14
    Grilled Halibut, 25
    Seared Yellowfin Tuna, 172
    Steamed Manila Clams, 144
fluke
    Sautéed Fluke, 159
frisée
    Roasted Haddock Filet, 61–62
frittata
    Smoked Salmon and Farm Egg
        Frittata, 38

G
garlic
    Baked Local Sole, 123
    Beer-Steamed Mussels, 148
    Garlic Prawns, 66
    Grilled Albacore, 167–168
    Grilled Halibut, 119
    Grilled Tuna Steak Frites, 87–88
    Pan-Fried Petrale Sole, 73
    Pan-Roasted Tru Cod, 31–32
    Poached Albacore Salad, 95
    Rosé-Steamed Clams, 7
    Salt Cod Croquettes, 79–80
    Sautéed Wild King Salmon, 43
    Skillet-Roasted Trout, 81–83
    Smoked Sockeye Salmon, 171
    Whole Roasted Dungeness Crab, 151
Garlic Prawns, 66
gherkins
    Rock Shrimp Po' Boy, 156
ginger
    Almond Milk–Poached Rock Cod, 77
    Champagne-Poached Sole, 26
    Ginger and Asparagus Soup, 91
    Grilled Albacore, 167–168
    Seared Yellowfin Tuna, 44
    Shandy-Steamed Steamer Clams, 104
    Shrimp and Coconut Soup, 116
    Smoked Sockeye Salmon, 171
    Sweet Potato and Ginger Tarte, 176
ginger, pickled
    Champagne-Poached Sole, 26
Ginger and Asparagus Soup, 91
grapefruit
    Seared Yellowfin Tuna, 172
    Steamed Manila Clams, 144
grapefruit juice
    Oysters on the Half Shell, 4
grapeseed oil
    Pan-Roasted Rock Cod, 165–166

Rock Shrimp Po' Boy, 156

Smoked Trout Salad, 131

green goddess dressing

Chilled Poached Salmon, 85–86

greens

Chilled Poached Salmon, 85–86

Grilled Albacore, 167–168

Grilled Day-Boat Scallops, 163

Grilled Halibut, 25, 70, 119, 160

Grilled Prawn Salad, 112

Grilled Scallops, 107

Grilled Tuna Steak Frites, 87–88

Grilled Wild King Salmon, 128

H

haddock

Roasted Haddock Filet, 61–62

halibut

Grilled Halibut, 25, 70, 119, 160

hazelnut oil

Grilled Scallops, 107

honey

Roasted Haddock Filet, 61–62

Seared Yellowfin Tuna, 44

Sweet Corn and Blueberry Pound
Cake, 136

horseradish

Oysters on the Half Shell, 4

Pan-Roasted Rock Cod, 165–166

hot sauce

Seared Yellowfin Tuna, 44

J

jalapeño

Roasted Haddock Filet, 61–62

K

kale

Pan-Roasted Tru Cod, 31–32

L

leeks

Ginger and Asparagus Soup, 91

Rosé-Steamed Clams, 7

Shrimp and Coconut Soup, 116

Steamed Mussel Chowder, 108

lemon

Lemon Sole Schnitzel, 29

Whole Roasted Dungeness Crab, 151

Whole Steamed Dungeness Crab, 16

lemonade

Shandy-Steamed Steamer Clams, 104

lemongrass

Shrimp and Coconut Soup, 116

Lemon Sole Schnitzel, 29

lemon verbena

Pan-Seared Tru Cod, 124

lettuce

Chilled Poached Salmon, 85–86

Rock Shrimp Po' Boy, 156

Salmon Burgers, 132

Soft-Shell Crab BLT, 65

lime

Sweet Corn and Blueberry Pound
Cake, 136

Whole Roasted Fish Taco Bar, 179

lime curd

Upside Down Pineapple Cake, 47

ling cod

Sautéed Ling Cod, 33–34

lobster

Chilled Lobster and Udon Noodle, 69

Poached Lobster, 111

Poached Maine Lobster, 21–22

Lobster Mac 'n Cheese, 155

Local Sand Dabs, 74

M

mango

Grilled Prawn Salad, 112

marjoram
  Pan-Fried Petrale Sole, 73
  Smoked Trout Salad, 131
mayonnaise
  Soft-Shell Crab BLT, 65
melon
  Oyster Ceviche, 103
milk
  almond
      Almond Milk–Poached Rock Cod,
        77
      Salt Cod Croquettes, 79–80
  Grilled Albacore, 167–168
  Sautéed Ling Cod, 33–34
mint
  Clams on the Half Shell, 54
  Ginger and Asparagus Soup, 91
  Grilled Halibut, 70
  Grilled Prawn Salad, 112
  Oyster Ceviche, 103
  Poached Maine Lobster, 21–22
  Seared Day-Boat Scallops, 8
  Timeless Tuna Tartare, 135
  Tuna Sashimi, 175
molasses
  Smoked Sockeye Salmon, 171
mushrooms
  Pan-Roasted Tru Cod, 31–32
  Shrimp and Coconut Soup, 116
mussels
  Beer-Poached Mussels, 11–12
  Beer-Steamed Mussels, 148
  Chilled Mussel Tea Sandwiches, 59–60
  Steamed Mussel Chowder, 108
mustard
  Champagne-Poached Sole, 26
  Grilled Halibut, 119
  Grilled Prawn Salad, 112
  Poached Albacore Salad, 95
  Salmon Burgers, 132

  Salt Cod Croquettes, 79–80
  Seared Yellowfin Tuna, 44
  Smoked Trout Salad, 131
  Whole Steamed Dungeness Crab, 16
mustard greens
  Pan-Fried Petrale Sole, 73

N
Napa cabbage
  Grilled Prawn Salad, 112
  Whole Roasted Fish Taco Bar, 179
noodles
  Chilled Lobster and Udon Noodle, 69
nutmeg
  Smoked Sockeye Salmon, 171

O
olives
  Baked Local Sole, 123
  Beer-Poached Mussels, 11–12
onion
  red
      Barbecued Oysters, 143
      Day-Boat Scallop Ceviche, 56
      Creole Gulf Prawns, 19–20
      Grilled Day-Boat Scallops, 163
      Grilled Halibut, 119
      Oyster Ceviche, 103
      Poached Maine Lobster, 21–22
      Timeless Tuna Tartare, 135
      Tuna Sashimi, 175
      Whole Roasted Fish Taco Bar, 179
      Yellowfin Tuna Ceviche, 41
  spring
      Grilled Halibut, 70
  Vidalia
      Roasted Haddock Filet, 61–62
  yellow
      Chilled Poached Salmon, 85–86
      Ginger and Asparagus Soup, 91

201

Lobster Mac 'n Cheese, 155
Pan-Roasted Tru Cod, 31–32
Shrimp and Coconut Soup, 116
Steamed Mussel Chowder, 108
orange. *See also* clementines
blood
Pan-Roasted Rock Cod, 165–166
Crispy Arctic Char, 13–14
Garlic Prawns, 66
orange juice
Crispy Arctic Char, 13–14
Oysters on the Half Shell, 4
Rhubarb and Strawberry Crisp, 96
oregano
Baked Local Sole, 123
Creole Gulf Prawns, 19–20
Grilled Halibut, 119
Grilled Wild King Salmon, 128
Pan-Roasted Rock Cod, 165–166
Pan-Seared Tru Cod, 124
Rosé-Steamed Clams, 7
Skillet-Roasted Trout, 81–83
Whole Roasted Fish Taco Bar, 179
Oyster Ceviche, 103
oysters
Baked Oysters, 53
Barbecued Oysters, 143
Oysters on the Half Shell, 4

P
Pacific tru cod
Pan-Roasted Tru Cod, 31–32
pancetta
Chilled Mussel Tea Sandwiches, 59–60
Pan-Fried Petrale Sole, 73, 120
panko
Lemon Sole Schnitzel, 29
Lobster Mac 'n Cheese, 155
Soft-Shell Crab BLT, 65
Pan-Roasted Prawns, 152

Pan-Roasted Rock Cod, 165–166
Pan-Roasted Tru Cod, 31–32
Pan-Seared Tru Cod, 124
parsley
Almond Milk–Poached Rock Cod, 77
Chilled Poached Salmon, 85–86
Day-Boat Scallop Ceviche, 56
Creole Gulf Prawns, 19–20
Crispy Arctic Char, 13–14
Grilled Halibut, 70, 119
Lemon Sole Schnitzel, 29
Pan-Fried Petrale Sole, 73
Pan-Roasted Prawns, 152
Poached Albacore Salad, 95
Poached Lobster, 111
Poached Maine Lobster, 21–22
Rosé-Steamed Clams, 7
Salmon Burgers, 132
Salt Cod Croquettes, 79–80
Sautéed Ling Cod, 33–34
Sautéed Wild King Salmon, 43
Shrimp and Coconut Soup, 116
Smoked Trout Salad, 131
Whole Steamed Dungeness Crab, 16
pasilla pepper
Pan-Fried Petrale Sole, 120
pasta
Beer-Poached Mussels, 11–12
Lobster Mac 'n Cheese, 155
Pan-Roasted Prawns, 152
peanuts, honey-roasted
Seared Day-Boat Scallops, 8
pear
Seared Yellowfin Tuna, 172
Sweet Potato and Ginger Tarte, 176
Yellowfin Tuna Ceviche, 41
peas
Clams on the Half Shell, 54
Grilled Halibut, 70

snow
>Chilled Poached Salmon, 85–86

pea tendrils
>Grilled Halibut, 119
>Poached Albacore Salad, 95

Pernod
>Baked Oysters, 53

pickles
>Dungeness Crab Rolls, 115
>Rock Shrimp Po' Boy, 156

pineapple
>Bay Scallop Fish Tacos, 147
>Grilled Halibut, 160
>Timeless Tuna Tartare, 135
>Upside Down Pineapple Cake, 47

pine nuts
>Pan-Roasted Tru Cod, 31–32

pistachios
>Grilled Halibut, 25
>Local Sand Dabs, 74

Poached Albacore Salad, 95

Poached Lobster, 111

Poached Maine Lobster, 21–22

pomegranate
>Grilled Halibut, 25

potatoes
>Almond Milk–Poached Rock Cod, 77
>Crispy Arctic Char, 13–14
>Grilled Halibut, 25, 70
>Grilled Tuna Steak Frites, 87–88
>Lemon Sole Schnitzel, 29
>Poached Lobster, 111
>Salt Cod Croquettes, 79–80
>Steamed Mussel Chowder, 108
>sweet potato
>>Sweet Potato and Ginger Tarte, 176
>Whole Roasted Dungeness Crab, 151
>Whole Steamed Dungeness Crab, 16
>Yellowfin Tuna Ceviche, 41

prawns
>Creole Gulf Prawns, 19–20
>Garlic Prawns, 66
>Grilled Prawn Salad, 112
>Pan-Roasted Prawns, 152

pretzels
>Grilled Albacore, 167–168

prosciutto
>Beer-Poached Mussels, 11–12

pumpkin seeds
>Seared Yellowfin Tuna, 172

R

radicchio
>Chilled Lobster and Udon Noodle, 69

radishes
>Chilled Lobster and Udon Noodle, 69
>French breakfast, 81–83

remoulade
>Rock Shrimp Po' Boy, 156

Rhubarb and Strawberry Crisp, 96

rice
>Champagne-Poached Sole, 26
>Creole Gulf Prawns, 19–20
>Ginger and Asparagus Soup, 91
>Shrimp and Coconut Soup, 116

rice paper
>Day-Boat Scallop Ceviche, 56

Roasted Haddock Filet, 61–62

Rock Shrimp Po' Boy, 156

Rosé-Steamed Clams, 7

rum
>Smoked Trout Salad, 131

S

sage
>Pan-Roasted Prawns, 152
>Sautéed Ling Cod, 33–34

salad
>Grilled Prawn Salad, 112
>Poached Albacore Salad, 95

salmon
    Chilled Poached Salmon, 85–86
    Grilled Wild King Salmon, 128
    Sautéed Wild King Salmon, 43
    smoked
        Smoked Salmon and Farm Egg
           Frittata, 38
        Smoked Sockeye Salmon, 171
Salmon Burgers, 132
salsa
    Grilled Day-Boat Scallops, 163
Salt Cod Croquettes, 79–80
sand dabs
    Local Sand Dabs, 74
sashimi
    Tuna Sashimi, 175
sausage
    Beer-Steamed Mussels, 148
Sautéed Fluke, 159
Sautéed Ling Cod, 33–34
Sautéed Wild King Salmon, 43
scallions
    Day-Boat Scallop Ceviche, 56
    Salmon Burgers, 132
    Sautéed Fluke, 159
scallops
    Bay Scallop Fish Tacos, 147
    Day-Boat Scallop Ceviche, 56
    Grilled Day-Boat Scallops, 163
    Grilled Scallops, 107
    Seared Day-Boat Scallops, 8
Seared Day-Boat Scallops, 8
Seared Yellowfin Tuna, 44, 172
seltzer
    Chilled Poached Salmon, 85–86
    Clams on the Half Shell, 54
sesame oil
    Timeless Tuna Tartare, 135
    Tuna Sashimi, 175
    Yellowfin Tuna Ceviche, 41

sesame seeds
    Tuna Sashimi, 175
shallots
    Beer-Poached Mussels, 11–12
    Beer-Steamed Mussels, 148
    Champagne-Poached Sole, 26
    Chilled Mussel Tea Sandwiches,
      59–60
    Ginger and Asparagus Soup, 91
    Grilled Albacore, 167–168
    Grilled Halibut, 119
    Grilled Scallops, 107
    Grilled Tuna Steak Frites, 87–88
    Oysters on the Half Shell, 4
    Pan-Fried Petrale Sole, 120
    Pan-Roasted Prawns, 152
    Pan-Roasted Rock Cod, 165–166
    Pan-Roasted Tru Cod, 31–32
    Roasted Haddock Filet, 61–62
    Rosé-Steamed Clams, 7
    Sautéed Ling Cod, 33–34
    Shrimp and Coconut Soup, 116
    Skillet-Roasted Trout, 81–83
    Smoked Trout Salad, 131
    Steamed Manila Clams, 144
    Steamed Mussel Chowder, 108
Shandy-Steamed Steamer Clams, 104
sherry vinegar
    Grilled Day-Boat Scallops, 163
    Grilled Halibut, 119
    Pan-Roasted Tru Cod, 31–32
    Roasted Haddock Filet, 61–62
    Whole Roasted Fish Taco Bar, 179
shishito peppers
    Grilled Day-Boat Scallops, 163
shrimp
    Creole Gulf Prawns, 19–20
    Garlic Prawns, 66
    Ginger and Asparagus Soup, 91
    Grilled Prawn Salad, 112

Pan-Roasted Prawns, 152
Rock Shrimp Po' Boy, 156
Shrimp and Coconut Soup, 116
Skillet-Roasted Trout, 81–83
Smoked Salmon and Farm Egg Frittata, 38
Smoked Sockeye Salmon, 171
Smoked Trout Salad, 131
snow peas
    Chilled Poached Salmon, 85–86
Soft-Shell Crab BLT, 65
sole
    Baked Local Sole, 123
    Champagne-Poached Sole, 26
    Lemon Sole Schnitzel, 29
    Pan-Fried Petrale Sole, 73, 120
soup
    Ginger and Asparagus Soup, 91
    Steamed Mussel Chowder, 108
sour cream
    Sautéed Fluke, 159
    Smoked Salmon and Farm Egg
        Frittata, 38
    Smoked Sockeye Salmon, 171
    Whole Roasted Fish Taco Bar, 179
soy sauce
    Chilled Lobster and Udon Noodle, 69
    Salmon Burgers, 132
    Timeless Tuna Tartare, 135
    Yellowfin Tuna Ceviche, 41
spinach
    Baked Oysters, 53
spring onions
    Grilled Halibut, 70
squash
    Grilled Albacore, 167–168
    Sautéed Ling Cod, 33–34
squid
    Skillet-Roasted Trout, 81–83
Steamed Manila Clams, 144
Steamed Mussel Chowder, 108

strawberries
    Rhubarb and Strawberry Crisp, 96
    Sweet Corn and Blueberry Pound
        Cake, 136
summer melon
    Oyster Ceviche, 103
sunflower seeds
    Grilled Halibut, 160
Sweet Corn and Blueberry Pound Cake,
    136
sweet potato
    Sweet Potato and Ginger Tarte, 176
Sweet Potato and Ginger Tarte, 176

T
Tabasco
    Seared Yellowfin Tuna, 44
tacos
    Bay Scallop Fish Tacos, 147
    Whole Roasted Fish Taco Bar, 179
tangerines
    Seared Yellowfin Tuna, 44
tarragon
    Beer-Poached Mussels, 11–12
    Champagne-Poached Sole, 26
    Chilled Poached Salmon, 85–86
    Grilled Albacore, 167–168
    Lobster Mac 'n Cheese, 155
    Seared Yellowfin Tuna, 44
    Steamed Manila Clams, 144
tarte
    Sweet Potato and Ginger Tart, 176
Thai basil
    Pan-Seared Tru Cod, 124
thyme
    Beer-Poached Mussels, 11–12
    Beer-Steamed Mussels, 148
    Champagne-Poached Sole, 26
    Chilled Mussel Tea Sandwiches, 59–60
    Chilled Poached Salmon, 85–86

Grilled Halibut, 70
Grilled Tuna Steak Frites, 87–88
Grilled Wild King Salmon, 128
Oysters on the Half Shell, 4
Roasted Haddock Filet, 61–62
Sautéed Ling Cod, 33–34
Timeless Tuna Tartare, 135
tomatoes
Grilled Day-Boat Scallops, 163
Grilled Halibut, 119
Grilled Wild King Salmon, 128
Pan-Seared Tru Cod, 124
Rock Shrimp Po' Boy, 156
Salmon Burgers, 132
Skillet-Roasted Trout, 81–83
Smoked Salmon and Farm Egg
Frittata, 38
Soft-Shell Crab BLT, 65
Whole Roasted Fish Taco Bar, 179
tomato paste
Grilled Halibut, 119
tomato sauce
Pan-Fried Petrale Sole, 120
tortillas
Bay Scallop Fish Tacos, 147
Whole Roasted Fish Taco Bar, 179
trout
Skillet-Roasted Trout, 81–83
Smoked Trout Salad, 131
tru cod
Pan-Roasted Tru Cod, 31–32
Pan-Seared Tru Cod, 124
tuna
Grilled Albacore, 167–168
Grilled Tuna Steak Frites, 87–88
Poached Albacore Salad, 95
Seared Yellowfin Tuna, 44, 172
Timeless Tuna Tartare, 135

Yellowfin Tuna Ceviche, 41
Yellowfin Tuna Crudo, 92
Tuna Sashimi, 175

U
udon noodles
Chilled Lobster and Udon Noodle, 69
Upside Down Pineapple Cake, 47

V
vinegar
balsamic
Baked Local Sole, 123
Grilled Halibut, 25
champagne
Baked Local Sole, 123
Chilled Mussel Tea Sandwiches,
59–60
Chilled Poached Salmon, 85–86
Grilled Prawn Salad, 112
Grilled Wild King Salmon, 128
Rock Shrimp Po' Boy, 156
Salt Cod Croquettes, 79–80
Sautéed Wild King Salmon, 43
Skillet-Roasted Trout, 81–83
Smoked Sockeye Salmon, 171
Smoked Trout Salad, 131
red wine
Grilled Tuna Steak Frites, 87–88
Pan-Fried Petrale Sole, 120
Pan-Roasted Rock Cod,
165–166
Poached Albacore Salad, 95
Sautéed Ling Cod, 33–34
sherry
Grilled Day-Boat Scallops, 163
Grilled Halibut, 119
Pan-Roasted Tru Cod, 31–32

Roasted Haddock Filet, 61–62
Whole Roasted Fish Taco Bar, 179
white wine
    Poached Maine Lobster, 21–22
    Sautéed Fluke, 159
    Whole Steamed Dungeness
       Crab, 16
    Yellowfin Tuna Ceviche, 41

W

watercress
    Salt Cod Croquettes, 79–80
    Sautéed Ling Cod, 33–34
    Skillet-Roasted Trout, 81–83
    Yellowfin Tuna Crudo, 92
Whole Roasted Dungeness Crab, 151
Whole Roasted Fish Taco Bar, 179
Whole Steamed Dungeness Crab, 16
wine
    Beer-Poached Mussels, 11–12
    Champagne-Poached Sole, 26
    Chilled Mussel Tea Sandwiches, 59–60
    Chilled Poached Salmon, 85–86
    Creole Gulf Prawns, 19–20
    Crispy Arctic Char, 13–14
    Garlic Prawns, 66

Ginger and Asparagus Soup, 91
Grilled Albacore, 167–168
Grilled Halibut, 70, 119
Grilled Tuna Steak Frites, 87–88
Lobster Mac 'n Cheese, 155
Rosé-Steamed Clams, 7
Sautéed Ling Cod, 33–34
Shrimp and Coconut Soup, 116
Steamed Manila Clams, 144
Steamed Mussel Chowder, 108
Worcestershire sauce
    Salmon Burgers, 132

Y

yellowfin tuna
    Grilled Tuna Steak Frites, 87–88
    Seared Yellowfin Tuna, 172
    Timeless Tuna Tartare, 135
    Yellowfin Tuna Ceviche, 41
Yellowfin Tuna Ceviche, 41
Yellowfin Tuna Crudo, 92

Z

zucchini
    Baked Local Sole, 123

conversion charts

METRIC AND IMPERIAL CONVERSIONS

(These conversions are rounded for convenience)

Ingredient	Cups/Tablespoons/ Teaspoons	Ounces	Grams/Milliliters
Butter	1 cup/ 16 tablespoons/ 2 sticks	8 ounces	230 grams
Cheese, shredded	1 cup	4 ounces	110 grams
Cream cheese	1 tablespoon	0.5 ounce	14.5 grams
Cornstarch	1 tablespoon	0.3 ounce	8 grams
Flour, all-purpose	1 cup/1 tablespoon	4.5 ounces/0.3 ounce	125 grams/8 grams
Flour, whole wheat	1 cup	4 ounces	120 grams
Fruit, dried	1 cup	4 ounces	120 grams
Fruits or veggies, chopped	1 cup	5 to 7 ounces	145 to 200 grams
Fruits or veggies, puréed	1 cup	8.5 ounces	245 grams
Honey, maple syrup, or corn syrup	1 tablespoon	.75 ounce	20 grams
Liquids: cream, milk, water, or juice	1 cup	8 fluid ounces	240 milliliters
Oats	1 cup	5.5 ounces	150 grams
Salt	1 teaspoon	0.2 ounce	6 grams
Spices: cinnamon, cloves, ginger, or nutmeg (ground)	1 teaspoon	0.2 ounce	5 milliliters
Sugar, brown, firmly packed	1 cup	7 ounces	200 grams
Sugar, white	1 cup/1 tablespoon	7 ounces/0.5 ounce	200 grams/12.5 grams
Vanilla extract	1 teaspoon	0.2 ounce	4 grams

OVEN TEMPERATURES

Fahrenheit	Celsius	Gas Mark
225°	110°	¼
250°	120°	½
275°	140°	1
300°	150°	2
325°	160°	3
350°	180°	4
375°	190°	5
400°	200°	6
425°	220°	7
450°	230°	8